A Decided Difference

A Decided Difference

LouAnn Watkins Clark

ISBN: 978-1-950721-11-5

Dedication

For Emily Caroline
and Katherine Whitney,
the lights of my life

Contents

Introduction

S o, what is a decided difference anyway? In common use, it means a major difference between two things, a difference that is readily noticeable, significant, and/or meaningful. It's the obvious visual difference between black and white. It's the temperature difference between the equator and the North Pole. It's the contrast that gives us so much pleasure in looking at before and after pictures. I think of it as that kind of pronounced difference with an added dimension. It is a difference *you* choose and create for yourself, because *you decided* to do it.

My own decided difference was choosing to find a lasting way to overcome depression and anxiety. My thinking, my moods, and my life have been decidedly different from the day I made that decision. You may have a similar challenge. Or perhaps you want to stop doubting yourself, stop feeling afraid to move forward, or finally live the life of your dreams. When you change your habits of thinking, you can achieve all of these things and more.

How powerful are the methods you will learn in this book? Consider my personal story.

I suffered from anxiety and depression for approximately twenty years. During that time, I participated in psychotherapy and also took various antidepressant medicines. I had been taking medications off and on for a dozen years when I realized I was in an unending spiral that had become dismally predictable. When I slid into depression, I felt more and more down, sad, and hopeless. I saw my doctor, who prescribed an antidepressant. Within days or weeks of starting the drug, I felt better. I had more energy, slept better, and felt more optimistic. I enjoyed life more. But as the months went by, different symptoms developed that were nearly as distressing as the depression had been. I was hungry all the time, or my stomach stayed upset. I felt restless and anxious. I lost interest in sex. Sleep became more elusive, and when I did sleep, I had strange and disturbing dreams. I took a few of the drugs for just a short time, because they made me too nauseated to function or gave me terrible headaches. After taking one of the drugs long term, I started having thoughts about how I would kill myself, if I were to decide to kill myself, which I would never do. Does that sound like disordered thinking? That's because it is. Fortunately, I recognized those thoughts were not typical of me, and when I stopped the drug, those thoughts also stopped. Since I have been off antidepressants, I have had no thoughts of suicide.*

In April 2003, I decided to stop taking antidepressant

medication. I was determined to end the cycle and find a better way to manage my moods. It was a terrifying decision. Even though I was afraid to stop relying on external manipulation of my brain chemistry to prop me up, something inside me said there had to be a better way, and I had to find it. I am happy to report I did.

This book is my attempt to share what I have learned and to provide you with the tools and techniques I personally use. These are methods you can use to effect any kind of change you want in your life: feeling happier and more in control of your moods, becoming physically healthier, creating a career you love. These techniques can make you a better friend, a better parent, or even a better golfer, if that is what lights you up. They are designed to help you live the life you want and to live it in a happier way.

I also want to give you the encouragement to continue using the tools once you understand them. Keeping your thoughts healthy and helpful is not an easy task. Negativity is a constant drumbeat in our world, present in all forms of media and interpersonal communications.

By the way, this is not just another book about positive thinking. I believe in positive thinking only when it is based in reality and appropriate to the situation. My self-talk, what I say when I talk to myself, needs to be truthful. I can say positive affirmations over and over, wishing they were true, but I know when I'm lying, every single time. So do you. Positive self-talk doesn't have to be airy-fairy, pie in the sky, magical thinking. I believe positive change is possible without unrealistic positive thinking. In fact, I think change becomes even more likely when pretense is not part of the package.

A caveat: I am not a medical professional nor a mental health professional. I am not a doctor, psychologist, social worker, nor counselor. But I am well-versed in how to change your thinking to be mentally healthier and to get what you want out of life. I am devoted to the practice of happiness. The techniques I recommend can be used whether you use medication or not. Please seek the advice of your own doctor to determine whether medication is right for you.

I want to emphasize that my choice to forgo taking medication was a personal decision, one I made for myself after a consultation with my doctor. I am not saying that taking drugs prescribed by your doctor is bad. I am not advising you to stop taking antidepressants or anti-anxiety drugs. Again, I am not a medical or mental health professional. Please remember that this book does not contain medical advice.

Choosing happiness is not simply about taking selfishly. It is about being healthy in a way that allows you to give as well as receive. The better way I have found is about choosing thoughts which serve and support me, both personally and in my relationships and roles with others. I have learned that our thoughts create our feelings, even when we are unaware of the process. Our feelings grow from our thoughts in the moment, and our attitudes grow from our patterns of thinking. I learned we do not have to be ruled by our moods, because thinking is a skill, one that is learned and can be deliberately practiced and improved.

I examined how I learned to think and discovered my thought patterns were not helping me create the life I wanted. In fact, my thoughts were crippling me. They were keeping me sad, stuck, and spiritless. I learned I could grow and change through conscious choice and action. The tools I use are simple, and they can be used by anyone. It takes dedication and practice to carry out the decision to be happy, especially in a world as seemingly threatening as today's is. But I truly believe if I can do it, you can, too. As I always say at the end of my podcast episodes, the world doesn't change. You do.

I have found the results to be well worth the effort. I hope you will, too.

—LouAnn Clark
Franklin, Tennessee
March, 2020

*The topic of suicide is outside the scope of this book, however. Please, if you have any thoughts of suicide, reach out for help immediately. Call your doctor, your therapist, or a friend who will help. Call the National Suicide Prevention Lifeline at 1-800-273-8255. It's free and confidential.

— Chapter 1 —

Change Is Possible

I f you have been waiting for permission to be happy, here it is. It is yours. Take it. It is time.

That's right. You have permission right now to do things that make your heart sing and to stop doing things that drain and bore you. I know—it's a radical thought. I'm having a stress-triggered hot flash just from writing it down. You deserve, as much as anyone, to be happy and to live a fulfilling life. I want you to take permission right now! Make the decision to be happy, and use every trick in this book to support your decision.

I decided to be happy, and it is by far the best decision I ever made. My life changed dramatically. The life I live today bears little resemblance to my life before the decision. I don't even look like the same person. You might expect that, given how many years have passed, but soon after I made my decision, an old friend mistook me for my daughter. Fifteen years later, it happened again. Feeling happy, alive, and in control of your life is the real fountain of youth.

It has not always been like that. Look back with me to when I thought I was doing everything I could to fight the depression which had dogged me for years. I found a good counselor and faithfully attended my therapy sessions. I consulted with a doctor I trusted and dutifully took the antidepressants he prescribed. I read everything I could get my hands on about depression and anxiety. I sometimes felt better, but I never felt on top of the thing called depression.

Well, how could I be expected to get on top of it? I was a depressive type, after all. I had Major Depression, according to the psychological standards contained in the DSM-IIIR, the diagnostic manual in use by mental health professionals at the time. I probably had Generalized Anxiety Disorder as well. I had felt down off and on since I was a freshman in high school, and the downs only got worse after graduation. I worried a lot, about practically everything. I did not cope well with the challenges of young adulthood. I probably had postpartum depression after the birth of both my children. Although much of the time I managed reasonably well on the outside, on the inside, I felt like a mess. I had come to believe things would never get very much better.

According to the research I read, I was doomed to struggle with depression and anxiety forever. I had both the genetic makeup and the environmental conditioning to practically guarantee it. Lots of members of my family dealt with mood disorders. Among the problems and behaviors of just the relatives I knew personally, I saw depression repeatedly. I saw bipolar disorder, which at that time was commonly called being manic-depressive. There were hoarders on both sides of the family tree, a fear-based behavior I recognized as stemming from anxiety about the future. I was a full-fledged adult before I realized there were people in the world who didn't worry constantly. I sometimes joke that if worrying were an Olympic sport, my family would boast multiple generations of gold medalists. But being paralyzed by anxiety is no joke. My family also taught me many lessons about guilt and shame, contributing factors to depression and anxiety. Above all, I learned from family and culture that I must never put myself first or let others down.

I came to accept that depression and its partners, anxiety, guilt, and shame, would always be present in my life. I came to believe depression was a part of me, like my curly hair or my big feet. I might have days when I felt better, but the days when I felt worse would always come. I assumed if I didn't continue to treat the depression with drugs, I would never find long-term relief. I believed depression was like diabetes, a chronic condition which must be managed medically. I resigned myself to taking medication for the rest of my life.

There were just a couple of problems with that plan. The drugs frequently had side effects which made me feel worse than the depression did, and all of them lost effectiveness over time. I would try a new drug and feel hopeful when I got good results. I would stay on the drug until the side effects became intolerable or it stopped working. Then I would stop taking medication and slide back into depression. Cue the beginning of the repeating cycle. My doctor would prescribe another new drug; I would rinse and repeat.

But then the day came when I said, "Enough." I think of it now as the laundry room epiphany.

Is there a place in a house more mundane than a laundry room? No one goes into the laundry room for anything resembling fun. Certainly no one goes in there expecting something extraordinary to happen. Yet, something extraordinary and life changing did happen in my laundry room. I read something on a T-shirt which caused my thinking to change—and this change in thinking changed me forever.

I have no idea who first decided that printing words on clothing was a good way to express ideas, but clever sayings, writ large, are common in modern American clothing. The words that changed my life, however, were quite small. They weren't printed on the front of the shirt. They were printed on a tag, and they expressed a simple philosophy: "Do what you like. Like what you do." Anyone who has worn a Life is Good® T-shirt has seen them. I had seen them before, but for some reason, reading them this time made me break down in tears.

I had been doing a lot of thinking for a long time. I had not been truly happy for years, although I had spent a great deal of time, energy, and effort trying to be. On the surface, I had a good life, but I had come to realize I neither did what I liked nor liked what I did. Something had to change, or I was never going to be happy. While I believed in general that life is good, my own personal life was not any fun anymore. I spent most of my time making sure the lives of others were good. I took care of my children, my husband, my extended family, my friends, my church family. The list went on and on. Taking care of them did give me satisfaction in many ways. I loved them, and what is more important than love? But if you had asked me that particular morning what I personally liked, I could barely have answered the question.

I looked at that tiny tag for a long time. Its words were so simple, but I felt them profoundly. I would probably never completely know the ultimate meaning of life, but at that moment, I realized serving others at the expense of my own joy was wrong. I knew I wasn't asking for much. I just wanted to choose the movie or the meal and not have someone second-guess my choice. I wanted to put myself first, not all the time, but at least once in a while. I didn't have to be at the top of my priority list, but I at least had to be on the list. Otherwise, I realized, I would come to the end of my life without having lived it.

Maybe changing my life based on T-shirt philosophy was a little weird. But of course, it wasn't really the marketing slogan on the T-shirt that changed things. It was my decision to accept the simple truth. My life was worth changing. If you don't do what you like and like what you do, maybe it's time for you to start.

Where do you begin? There is only one option: begin wherever you happen to be.

It was easy to decide things had to change. But it was not as easy to figure out how to make the changes and make them stick. I had to start somewhere, so I decided to consult my counselor. Jim is a caring and capable man who operates from a base of kindness. In short, he is the type of counselor I wish everyone could have. He tried mightily to help me and my husband when we went for marriage counseling. Although it seemed things were not improving in our relationship, I still trusted Jim's ability to help me. I made an appointment to see him individually and told him about the laundry room epiphany. I lamented my struggles with depression and expressed my fears that I would never feel better. I had gone off another antidepressant medication, and while I didn't want to try a new one again, I feared I had no choice. Jim listened attentively, asked relevant questions, and spoke kindly as he offered suggestions. But I was still frustrated. Once again, I didn't seem to be getting anywhere with therapy.

Jim seemed to share my frustration. Maybe it was my story about not doing what I liked or liking what I did that prompted him to suddenly ask if he could just offer an unsolicited opinion. "Please!" I readily agreed. I was eager to consider anything that might help pull me out of that dark place.

That is when Jim spoke the simple words that changed everything. "LouAnn," he said, "I don't think you have clinical depression. I don't think you have an anxiety disorder. I think any normal person living in your circumstances would feel depressed."

At first glance, this may not sound like an earth-shattering difference. Yet I instantly knew what he said would cause a profound shift in the way I saw myself. I had come to believe I was a depressed person. I believed I was mentally ill, which meant I was sick, defective, and abnormal. If only my depression could be fixed, then everything would be fine. But I believed I was hopelessly unfixable. I was flawed, inadequate, unhealthy. There was no cure. When Jim shared his professional opinion that I was a normal person, dealing with external circumstances which made me feel depressed, I felt like a prison door had swung open. Suddenly, I was free to walk out into the sunshine with everyone else, because I was a normal woman. I just happened to have some challenging problems.

I have a friend who refers to experiences of sudden insight like this as lightning bolt moments. It fits. After being struck by lightning, you will never be the same.

Jim's words affirming the T-shirt tag message ignited the exploration that led me out of depression and into a life of happiness. I won't pretend it was easy or painless, because it was not. I got divorced. I lost some "friends." Many things changed, but eventually, I realized most of the changes were for the better. My life today is rich and full of true friends, more than ever before. My children, now adults, are thriving. I am looking forward to an awesome, opportunity-filled future while I enjoy the wonderful present.

I still have bad days sometimes, and I still have to work at keeping things positive. I would be mortified to give the impression that I am always happy-go-lucky and my life is all roses and sunshine. A new acquaintance recently said to me, "You seem like a happy soul." He didn't know I have to be proactive in keeping depression at bay, because for whatever reasons, I remain prone to it. Still, the effort is absolutely worthwhile.

Today, life is good. I do what I like, and I like what I do. I still serve others, but not at the expense of my own joy. Amazingly, when I nurture my own joy, it seems I have more abundant resources to share with others.

This book is my attempt to share what I have learned so that you may also nurture your own joy and give abundantly to those you care about. I have purposefully kept it short. This way, you can immediately take the tools I offer and put them into use. You don't have to do everything perfectly to get superb results. I have seen change happen before my very eyes when someone changes the way they think, and I have seen fabulous transformations when these techniques are practiced over time.

This book is meant to be used in the manner you might use a cookbook. The basic techniques remain the same, regardless of which dish you make. Once you know how to slice, dice, sauté, and simmer, you can use those skills to cook in any kitchen. I urge you to try everything for yourself. Some recipes will appeal to you, and some will not. Test these ideas out. Keep the ones that work for you, and please, do not feel like you are doing something wrong if some of them don't work. "Individual differences" is one of the terms psychologists use to explain getting varying results when using the same methods. You are an individual, and the mixture of methods that work for you will be personal.

Jim handed me the key that unlocked my prison door. Like any freed prisoner, though, I had to adjust to life on the outside, which took some effort. I want to offer you the key to your personal prison and accompany you as you take your path to freedom from negative emotions. The reward that lies ahead is worth the journey.

Beginning the Journey
Questions and Actions to Begin

- What makes you feel happy? Make a list of people, activities, places, events, and possessions that you enjoy. You don't have to justify any of them to anyone else. If you like it, you like it.
- How often do you do the things that make you feel happy and satisfied? How can you find ways to do them more often?
- Is there anything you enjoyed when you were younger that you stopped doing? Could you let yourself start doing it again? If not, what is stopping you?
- Consider the circumstances you are living in. Is there genuine pain underneath, even though things look good on the surface?
- Have you fallen into the habit of thinking of yourself as mentally ill or defective because of the way you feel? How would a "normal" person living in your circumstances feel?

— Chapter 2 —

The Key to the Prison

This book is not just for those who have been given a diagnosis of depression, anxiety, or another mood disorder. It is not just for those who struggle with negative thinking. If you are depressed and struggling, you can use the tools you find here to be happier. If you are already happy and thriving, you can also use the tools you find here to become even happier. Anyone who experiences occasional self-doubt, fear, or worry can benefit from using these techniques.

There are a few basic ideas you need to understand to take control of your own mind and your own mood. These are simple ideas, but their impact cannot be overstated.

1. Your thoughts create your feelings. Your moods and attitudes come from your thoughts.
2. Thinking is a skill, and skills are learned and

can be improved with practice. Therefore, thinking can be improved with practice.
3. You can deliberately choose what to think. You can *decide*.

Let's examine these ideas one at a time. First, your thoughts create your feelings, your moods, and your attitudes. I cannot emphasize this enough. We create our emotions in response to events in our lives. Our emotional lives are based on the stories we invent, consciously or subconsciously, about what those events mean. The human brain works full-time to make sense of the world, and study after study has demonstrated we will find or create explanations for whatever happens to us.

If you have never given much thought to your thinking, the chances are excellent that you are unconsciously creating these stories, and whatever you tell yourself, you believe. This is why I put so much emphasis on questioning ourselves about our "automatic" feelings. If I feel depressed and I keep telling myself, "I am depressed. There is nothing to feel happy about, the world is a terrible place, and life is so hard," I will continue to feel blue, down, and hopeless. On the other hand, if I deliberately look for the good things around me and cultivate gratitude for the many blessings in my life, I will feel secure, excited about life, and optimistic.

Simply questioning the stories we tell ourselves can make a real difference in how we feel. If we can consciously create alternate stories, we can feel much, much happier. By the way, these alternate explanations I favor are just as true as the automatic ones that pop into our heads. Alternate explanations don't necessarily have to include "positive thinking." I don't believe in positive thinking when it involves outright lying to yourself.

The things you choose to look for, to pay attention to, and to dwell upon have a great impact on how you feel. Much of the information in this book will focus on how to take deliberate control of these factors to create much happier results.

This leads us to consider the second basic idea: Thinking is a skill, and skills are learned and can be improved with practice.

Who taught you to think? Have you ever even considered this question? Thinking seems automatic. Thinking does become so after years of practice, the same way you can automatically brush your teeth or drive a car without much conscious attention. At one time, however, driving a car was difficult for you. You had to pay attention to every part of the experience, from steering and accelerating to stopping and backing up. You might still have to pay close attention when you parallel park or try to maneuver in a tight parking garage.

When you learned to think, you didn't pay any conscious attention to the process, because you simply couldn't. You were a baby, a toddler, a young child. By the time you were old enough to question your thinking, the patterns were set—not that it would have occurred to you to question them.

When you decide to change your thinking, it is like learning to drive. At first, you have to pay attention to lots of different things, but with practice, new habits will take over.

So who taught you to think the way you think? Your first teachers were the people who took care of you when you were a baby. Your inborn instinct was to imitate their behavior. You were not born with the ability to question whether or not their ways of thinking were healthy and rational. When you were a small child, you trusted the adults around you to teach you to make your way in the world. You had no other choice. You absorbed their attitudes about everything without questioning. The way your mother thought about herself and her place in the world affected you. The way your father or aunt or grandparents thought about you and your place in the world affected you. Everything they said and did had an impact on your thinking. Their attitudes about everything informed your thinking long before you had any idea what an attitude was, much less that there might be a different way.

Eventually, you went to school, and another layer of influence was laid down. The expectations of your teachers influenced you, even if neither they nor you were aware it was happening. The attitudes and expectations of peers also came into play. You were labeled and categorized at school. Which categories were you placed in? Were you labeled a jock, brainiac, class clown, or underachiever? These labels informed how you thought about yourself and helped create actions that matched the expectations others had about you.

Everywhere you went in your young life, the opinions of others formed the way you thought and how you saw yourself. Leaders at church, extended family, the parents of your friends, the friends of your parents, neighbors, sports coaches, Scout leaders . . . the list of influencers is endless. At some point, you probably started to disagree with some of the adults in your life. But that doesn't mean their influence on you ended.

Other factors in your environment also shaped the way you saw yourself. When I was growing up, one big impact was television, because it came right into our homes. Today, that influence has expanded with an endless variety of channels and has been joined by all types of online media. If you want to know what is (supposedly) right or wrong, good or bad, moral or immoral, and attractive or ugly, all you have to do is watch and listen.

So, did you learn to think the way you think deliberately or by accident? Are your thinking patterns and attitudes all your own, or are they a stew of the opinions, values, and expectations of others?

The most important question is this: Are your thoughts helping you to create the emotions, the actions, and the life you want? What you think is not necessarily a true reflection of reality, but your results will be a true reflection of your thoughts. The quality of your life depends upon the quality of your thoughts.

You may believe you can't control your thoughts or your moods, or that you are just at the mercy of whatever happens to you. This belief is the first thing you will need to change to think your way to a better life. Give it a fair chance. Be willing to try everything until something works. The techniques I suggest are not difficult, but you are the only you in the world. The combination of things that work or don't work for you will be unique. Furthermore, you may try a technique that doesn't work for you today, but when your basic ways of thinking have changed with time, you may have a different experience. One piece of advice I give consistently is to keep trying.

You can deliberately choose what to think. You can decide. When I first encountered this idea, it came wrapped in the complicated package of positive thinking. Napoleon Hill, the author of Think and Grow Rich, wrote, "Whatever the mind of man can conceive and believe, it can achieve." Doesn't that sound great in theory? It was the believing part that tripped me up. I didn't want to live in some fantasy world, lying to myself about how great things were. I also didn't believe deceiving myself would ultimately lead to the creation of whatever I was lying about. I still do not believe these things today. I have come to understand positive thinking can be a great tool, but there are also times when positive thinking can keep us stuck. Choosing your thoughts doesn't mean always being positive. Rather, it means being aware and conscious of the thoughts rattling around inside your head. It means questioning whether your thoughts are rational, realistic, or helpful. It means deciding to maintain awareness and change your thoughts whenever you realize they are not serving you. You can do all of these things without telling yourself a single lie.

I hope you are ready to question the way you think, reconsider the way you see yourself, and learn ways to choose better thoughts. By doing these things, you can live a happier, more successful life. It can start today.

Continuing the Journey
Questions and actions for moving forward

- Begin noticing what you are thinking when you experience negative feelings. Write down the things you are saying to yourself. Don't judge them, just begin to become aware.
- Who taught you to think? Make a list of the people whose opinions and attitudes influenced yours, for better or for worse.
- What are the labels you apply to yourself? Do you still identify with the labels given to you by others when you were younger? How do you fill in the blank in the sentence: "I am a(n)_____"?

— Chapter 3 —
Feeling Bad

Before you begin any change, it is a good idea to assess your starting point. Where are you now? What is your current reality? What is the state of your mind, your mood, your body, your job, your relationships, your health, your finances, your *life*?

Because you are reading this book, I am guessing you feel bad in some way. This could range from slight dissatisfaction with your current circumstances to the empty, hopeless feeling of deep depression. I will explore these so-called negative emotions in a moment, but first, let's take a minute for a reality check.

There are people who say nothing in the world is negative if you look at it in the proper way. I vehemently disagree. Yes, you may choose to make lemonade if life hands you lemons, but there is no denying you did not order lemons in the first place. There are also times when life gives you lemons that are rotten through and through.

When I encourage you to change your thinking, I am not suggesting you live in denial. Sometimes, the news really is bad and the pain really does hurt. If you are enjoying your trip to the mountains until you trip and fall into the campfire, no one would suggest you just lie there, trying to make the best of it. You want to pull yourself out of a situation like that as fast as you possibly can.

This is one reason I don't like the trend of prescribing antidepressant medication as a first line of defense for sad feelings, even persistent ones. Again, I am not a medical professional; this is just my opinion. Often there are other options which can be just as effective, not to mention less expensive and without the risk of unpleasant side effects.

I remember a certain Wednesday which was a really hard day. I won't share all the details, but let's just say it involved bad news involving a romantic relationship and more bad news involving money. I believed I had let a friend down, and I learned another dear friend was moving a thousand miles away. The afternoon ended with bad news from my dentist. It was nothing life threatening, but that was the tipping point. I couldn't help myself. I started to cry right there in the dental chair.

I am blessed to have as my dentist a man who is caring and compassionate. He immediately recognized there was more behind my tears than the news that my tooth couldn't be saved. He also knew one of my unconscious stress responses was to grind my teeth, and grinding my teeth was what killed the tooth that couldn't be saved. So he kindly offered to write a prescription for a little something, perhaps a low dose of a tranquilizer to help me relax, just for the short term. I immediately shook my head. When I told him I didn't take those drugs, he respected my decision. But he also said that in the short term, drugs to alleviate emotional distress can be helpful. I definitely agreed, but I was firm. I did not want them.

That is when he said something profound. He said, "The drugs can help you tolerate the stress. But sometimes, you end up putting up with things that you should not tolerate."

To put it in a somewhat vulgar fashion, this quotation lays it out bluntly: "Before you diagnose yourself with depression or low self-esteem, first make sure you are not, in fact, just surrounded by assholes." (The quotation is sometimes attributed to Sigmund Freud, but it originated much more recently. It was said by Twitter user Notorious d.e.b (@debihope). When the website https://quoteinvestigator.com/ asked how she came up with the idea, she said, "Popped right out of my own head and based on a past boyfriend." Oh, Notorious d.e.b., I hear you, girl!)

For the past several decades, a favorite theme in pop psychology has been the idea that no one is at fault. If you believe you are a victim, you are wrong, because you subconsciously participate in creating the abuse directed at you. If your spouse cheats on you, you must have done something to contribute to his or her choice. There must be problems in your relationship which are at least partially your fault. Criminals who victimize others are suffering from traumas in their histories and need understanding and treatment, not punishment. I could go on, but this line of thinking is making me feel sick to my stomach. I believe in taking responsibility for your own self, but I also believe if someone is hurting you, the best thing you can do is to take action to escape the situation.

The words you use to characterize negative emotions are important, whether you are talking to others or to yourself. When a friend says to me, "You seem depressed," I immediately disagree, even if I have not been feeling my best. For me, depression signifies a mental environment, a state, rather than a simple mood. Depression is pervasive and lasting, not something you can just shake off. I don't believe in using the word casually.

If you have been feeling disappointed or frustrated by certain events in your life, that is not depression. You may be going through a rough patch or facing challenges, but if you name it depression, you can make things harder for yourself.

When I was depressed, I didn't feel appropriate pleasure in hobbies, recreation, family life, or social interaction. The world seemed like a gray place, barren of joy. I didn't understand how others could happily go about their lives when everything seemed so pointless to me. I sometimes felt sad, but not always. Much of the time, I just felt empty and dull. Activities seemed to be more trouble than they were worth. Everything felt like work; life was an endless treadmill of one difficult task after another. Nothing felt very rewarding.

It is deeply unpleasant for me to remember these feelings, but doing so serves three purposes. One, it helps me to appreciate how good life feels these days. Two, it reminds me change is always possible. And three, remembering the pain of the depressed years reinforces my commitment to share a message of hope.

When you find yourself feeling "depressed," examine the feeling more closely. Ask yourself about the specifics. Are you grieving? Lonely? Frustrated? Overwhelmed? Consider the differences in coping with these feelings compared to "depression." Grief is unavoidable in this life, but it is actually a healthy response to loss. While it may never completely go away, its intensity wanes as time passes. Acceptance of the changed circumstances can eventually lead to feelings of peace. We can take specific steps to be more socially engaged and less lonely. Frustration cries out for solutions to particular problems. When we are overwhelmed, we have the option of setting priorities and saying no. We can find ways to deal with all kinds of negative feelings when we don't default to thinking it is depression, and subsequently think there is nothing we can do except medicate ourselves.

Changing your thinking does change your reality, and it begins by naming things appropriately. When you choose a label for your negative feeling that suggests a solution exists, it can be the first step toward finding the solution. You may have heard this idea expressed as "Name it to tame it."

What about anger? While feeling angry is not pleasant, I don't necessarily consider it an unhealthy negative emotion. Anger can move you to take action when action is needed. Some theories suggest depression is anger turned inward. I'll discuss anger in more detail later in the book.

American culture often sends the message that all

negative emotions are to be avoided. You may think if you don't feel happy all the time, you're somehow doing life wrong. I believe it is healthy to feel mad or sad or bad sometimes, because it can lead to needed changes in your thinking or your behavior. I see negative emotions as symptoms that something is wrong, either in your world or in your thinking. Because of this, I don't think avoidance is the answer.

You may be surprised to learn this, but I don't think the goal of feeling good all the time is a worthy one. I believe the path to happiness necessarily includes experiencing the emotions we call bad. In the real world, we sometimes have to go through unpleasantness in order to come out on the other side healthier, stronger, and more empowered to deal with whatever challenges come our way.

My daughter, Caroline, summed it up well when she talked about a big remodeling project she was doing in her century-old home. I said it could be awfully unpleasant to live in a house that was essentially under construction. She agreed, but she added, "In the long run, it will be less stressful to fix the house than to live in it without doing the renovations." It is the same with fixing our thinking. If you avoid confronting negative situations, whether they are inner or outer situations, you will experience far more stress in the long run. The short-term pain of confrontation can lead to long-term solutions.

When I look back on the years I spent in depression, the sadness isn't what I remember as the worst part of the suffering. Rather, it was the inability to feel joy and the lack of hope. While it wasn't pleasant to confront the errors in my thinking or the problems in my environment, plowing through those challenges ultimately renovated my life. The process was not fun, but the results were ultimately quite satisfying. I continue to reap the rewards of the work as I continue using the process today.

You don't have to be at the mercy of your emotions, whether they are "bad" or "good." You have more power and can exert more control over your feelings than you may believe.

Continuing the Journey
Questions and actions for moving forward

- Take stock of your starting point. How do you describe your mood? Your body? Your job or career? Your relationships? Your health? Your finances? Your specific areas of concern? Your life in general?
- Are you putting up with things that are not tolerable? What are they?
- Make a list of emotions you feel throughout the day, labeling your feelings in precise terms. If you feel sad, try being more specific. Are you heartbroken, lonely, bitter, or grieving? Using clear-cut terms for feelings can help you identify the thoughts that led to those feelings.
- Identify specific problems or issues you would like to address. Remember, naming them is the first step in taming them.

— Chapter 4 —

How Thoughts Create Feelings

How much do you think about the way you feel? Do you ever tell yourself you should feel a certain way, or you should *not* feel a certain way? Do you think feelings just come and go? Do you think emotions depend on external factors, such as events in your world or the passage of time?

There is at least one emotion which is instinctive and does not involve conscious thought: fear. I am talking about fear of things such as heights or lions or snakes. These fears are called adaptive, because they help keep us alive when we find ourselves in situations which are truly life threatening. This is the fear that makes your body react in the classic fight, flight, or freeze response, even though you have not given a conscious thought to the fear. Scientists have argued endlessly about how to define and categorize and classify emotions. But there is only one main thing you need to know to take control of your own emotional life: aside from instinctive fear, your feelings arise mainly from your thoughts.

Do you ever say to yourself, I should feel happy about this, or I should not feel guilty, or I should be ashamed, or I should not let this get to me? How about the perennial favorite, I should be over it by now?

I refer to should as the S-word, because using it causes us so much emotional pain and suffering. Whether you hear it from someone else or say it to yourself, "should" is a word that implies judgment, but at the same time, when it comes to feelings, it is essentially meaningless. Feelings are not something we should or should not have. Who gets to say how you should feel? Feelings happen as we consciously or unconsciously create our responses to events in our lives.

We assign meaning to external events, and our thoughts about that meaning create our feelings. We do the same thing with our thoughts about the past and the future. If meaning is involved, we can be sure we are telling ourselves stories about the significance of events, whether we are conscious of our creation of those stories or not. Once we become aware of the stories, we can choose to change them. As a result, the feelings may change a great deal as well. Or, maybe they don't change so much. Either way, whatever you are feeling, there is no should.

A feeling begins when something happens, either in the external world or inside your head. When you sense something through one of your physical senses—sight, hearing, smell, taste, or touch—your brain instantly interprets the meaning of the sensation. If you wake up in the morning and look out the window to see fresh snow, you will likely have an emotional response. If you love to play in snow, and you are an elementary school student, your emotional response will probably be delight—snow day! Your response will be quite different if you are the nurse who lives next door and is afraid to drive in snowy conditions but still has to go to work. The situation outside your windows is the same, but while one neighbor is rejoicing, another is filled with dread. If the fresh snow has fallen in April, just when you thought a long, hard winter had come to an end, you may feel frustrated, angry, or even hopeless, whether or not you have to go out in the snow.

Emotional responses like these happen in the tiniest fractions of a second. They happen whether we are paying conscious attention or not. They happen all day long, day in and day out, all through our lives. But that does not mean your thoughts have no bearing on how the emotions are created and sustained.

The best explanation for this process that I have come across is in Jill Bolte Taylor's book, My Stroke of Insight. The book is Taylor's account of her experiences during a stroke and her recovery from it. Under any circumstances, the story would be enlightening, but Taylor gives it an added dimension. She happens to be a Harvard-educated brain scientist.

She called one of the processes she observed during her recovery "the 90-second rule." It has to do with how the brain and the body respond to stress, and how feelings of stress can be perpetuated by the thoughts we choose. She explains that a physical chemical process is set into motion whenever we have an emotional reaction to something. Whether the stressful something is a close call on the highway, the diagnosis of a frightening illness, or the delivery of bad financial news, chemicals flood through your body in a response of fear or anger. Taylor says these stress chemicals remain in your system for only ninety seconds before they completely dissipate.

When was the last time you were afraid or angry for only a minute and a half? This is where your thoughts enter the picture.

For example, let's say a semi-truck suddenly swerves into your lane while you're going seventy miles per hour on the interstate. Without thinking, you instinctively veer onto the shoulder to miss the truck. Your heart is now racing; your pupils have dilated; your blood pressure has spiked. A part of your body called the autonomic nervous system has done all of this and more without your conscious involvement or consent. This is an automatic fear reaction, which triggers the physical chemical cascade that lasts for ninety seconds.

Look objectively at what happens a minute and a half later. The danger is over, at least from that single episode. You slowed down and merged back into traffic. The truck has barreled on down the highway, the driver perhaps oblivious that you were endangered by his carelessness. You are alive and well and still in control of your vehicle. Your hands have stopped shaking, as the last remnant of the rush of stress hormones has just finished coursing through your body. Do you now just forget about the near miss and turn your thoughts to what you will have for dinner? If you could do that, your body would relax into a normal, non-stressed state, and you would not continue to feel afraid or angry.

However, what happens if you continue to run angry thoughts through your mind? What if you keep thinking, "What a jerk! He nearly caused me to wreck! I could have been killed! He should have been paying attention. He's going to kill somebody if he keeps driving like that!" What if you replay the scene in your mind, visualizing again and again the trailer swerving over the line and nearly knocking your car off the road? What if you start thinking about how dangerous and unpredictable driving in heavy traffic can be, or about how so many people are driving distracted these days, or about how dangerous the world is in general?

If you think this way, you will continue to feel emotionally upset long after the triggering event is over. Your body will reflect that. The same circuits in your brain which responded to the initial fear are reactivated by your thoughts. Those circuits are joined by others as you continue retelling yourself a story about the wrongness of what happened. Stress hormones will continue to circulate in your system for as long as you dwell on the upsetting thoughts.

When you get home, if you tell your wife about the near accident, she may experience a similar rush of stress chemicals even though she was nowhere near the highway. It is only her thoughts and reactions to your story that have created her sensation of fear or anger, but the physiological response occurs in the same way.

Fear of physical harm is self-explanatory. It is sheer survival. When anything threatens your safety, fear is a healthy, normal response. When you are in fear, the autonomic nervous system activates your physical body systems to prepare you to take action: fight an attacker, run for your life, or quickly steer your sedan to the side of the road. Replaying thoughts of past dangers can be adaptive, because it can help you avoid or successfully cope with similar situations in the future. However, when you dwell upon thoughts of how weak and small you are compared to the dangers of the world, you can make yourself even weaker and less able to cope. More than that, you can construct a gloomy mental environment for yourself to live in every day.

Fortunately, the same brain which creates negative emotions in response to angry or fearful thoughts can also create positive emotions in the presence of happy thoughts. Imagine for a moment external events such as the aroma of your favorite cookies baking, the sound of your best friend laughing with delight, or the sight of your college-age child arriving at the local airport after a semester spent studying abroad. Your body also responds to these events, but in a much more enjoyable fashion. Think back to a time when you were filled with a flush of positive emotion, such as your wedding, the birth of a child, or the news that you got the job you really wanted. Think about how it felt when you got a new bicycle for Christmas or welcomed the arrival of a beloved family pet. Recall the pride you felt when you caught a fish with Grandpa or the exhilaration you felt the first time you got up on water skis. Try to re-experience the pleasant memory as though you had traveled back in time. Your brain circuits are lighting up again in a fashion very similar to when you actually experienced the event, and the same chemicals are being produced in your brain and body. Congratulations! You have just consciously created positive emotions and their physiological expression from nothing but pure thought.

You do this all the time, whether your thoughts are of fond memories of the past or anxious worries about the future. Your thoughts may be joyful appreciation of the present moment or red-hot anger in the present moment. Wherever your thoughts lead, your emotions will follow. This is very good news, because it means that by changing your thoughts, you can change the way you feel. You can take charge of your mind, and your heart will follow. If you do this, you can live a much happier and more satisfying life from now on.

When I first put the Decided Difference tools to work in my life, they seemed miraculous, but oh, so simple. I wondered how I could have lived more than four decades and not learned these methods. When I had been feeling better for some time, I started to feel a little down on myself for taking forever to figure this stuff out. It all seemed like common sense after a while. How could I have missed it?

I don't want you to fall into that same thinking trap. Your brain will have received more than a trillion bits of information in just the time it has taken you to read this sentence. Some of the information is processed by your brain, and some of it is ignored. And that's just considering the information coming in from the outside, through your senses. It does not include such things as language processing, using your imagination, or figuring out what to wear to your class reunion. The world is a complicated place, full of sensory information, facts, opinions, rules, manners, morals, and songs that repeat on endless replay in your head. There is also a phenomenon called the curse of knowledge, which is a quirk of the brain. Once you know something, it appears to be so obvious you think you should have known it all along. (Did you catch the S-word in the previous sentence?) Don't let the curse of knowledge become a reason to mentally beat yourself up.

It is highly unlikely anyone has taken the time to teach you to think in deliberate ways that serve and support you. Even if they had, they might have left out some important information. For one thing, we don't fully understand all the workings of the brain, and for another, your brain frequently does things without your awareness or your permission. Some of these things are useful. For example, I am glad I don't have to remember to breathe or beat my heart or open my sweat glands during summer in Tennessee. However, the brain also creates predictable errors in thinking, called cognitive biases, which are not so helpful. One that you are very familiar with is stereotyping of other people, notably those you perceive as different from you. Later in the book, I discuss common habits of thought that can be recognized and modified to your great advantage. For now, begin by understanding that not even the world's most brilliant neuroscientist is immune to these tricks played by the brain.

An important part of your mental functioning when it comes to mood is your belief system. I'm not talking here about religious or moral beliefs, but rather the things you think are true about yourself, the world, and your place in the world. As with cognitive biases, it is important to realize you have beliefs that developed without your conscious permission or participation. One belief of this type contributes greatly to depression. It is called "learned helplessness." I wish there were a better term for it, because even if you develop learned helplessness, you are not truly helpless. When you recognize and understand what happens in the process, you can not only overcome it, but you can exponentially increase both your personal feelings of power and your objective results. I know that is a big claim, but I also know I have experienced this myself.

The phenomenon of learned helplessness was discovered, as so many things are, by accident. In the late 1960s, Dr. Martin Seligman was participating in research conducted on dogs at the University of Pennsylvania. The work was inspired by the conditioning experiments carried out by Dr. Ivan Pavlov, which laid the foundation for learning theory. Seligman noticed some of the dogs in the experiments were behaving in unexpected ways. His investigation of their behavior led to the theory of learned helplessness, which has become a pillar of depression theory. (Seligman went on to help create the therapy method known as cognitive behavioral therapy, or CBT, and he became known as the father of positive psychology. At this writing, Seligman serves as director of Penn's Positive Psychology Center.)

So what is learned helplessness, and what does it have to do with you and me?

To illustrate the basic idea, I am going to simplify the story of his experiments, of which there were many.

Let me quickly say that, although the experiments which demonstrated learned helplessness involved subjecting dogs to electric shock, Martin Seligman doesn't hate dogs and doesn't like to hurt them. The shock was unpleasant but not dangerous.

Each dog was placed in a cage called a shuttle box, which had a floor made of a metal grid. The cage was divided in half, with a low barrier in the middle. The barrier was low enough for the dog to easily jump over. The dogs were divided into two groups, called conditions. Each group would be treated differently and their responses measured.

The first group of dogs was in the "escapable shock" condition. One side of the metal floor of the cage was electrified so a shock could be applied to the dog's paws. The dog could escape the shock by simply jumping over the low barrier, because the other side of the cage floor was not electrified. The dogs in this group quickly learned to jump to the safe side of the cage.

The second group of dogs were in the "inescapable shock" condition. When the floor of the cage was electrified and started to shock their paws, at first they also quickly jumped over the barrier in an attempt to escape the shock. Unfortunately for these dogs, the other side of the cage was also electrified. No matter where they went in the cage, they could not escape from the shocks.

The dogs were exposed to the experimental conditions multiple times, until they had learned the environment of the cage. Then the experimenters changed things up. All the dogs were now placed in the escapable shock condition; that is, all they had to do to escape the shock was to jump over the low barrier. How long do you think it took the dogs to learn that?

Naturally, the dogs who had always been able to escape the shock quickly jumped over the barrier to safety and stopped receiving the shocks. But here is where it gets strangely interesting. The dogs who had previously learned that both sides of the cage floor were electrified did not even try to escape the shock. They just stood there or even lay down on the electrified floor. They whimpered, but they just took the shock for its thirty-second duration, even though all they had to do to escape from it was to jump over the low barrier. They didn't even try.

Seligman was puzzled. Why was this happening? He theorized it happened because the dogs had learned they could not make a difference in their situations, no matter what they did. They had learned they had no control over what happened to them in the shuttle box. They had learned they were helpless to change their experience. They continued to behave the same way they had in the initial experiment, even though the conditions had changed. They stopped looking for a way to escape the shock, because they were certain nothing they tried would work. They had tried. They had failed. So they stopped trying, even though relief was mere inches away.

This is how even a dog can develop a belief that what it does makes no difference. Nothing it does matters, so it stops trying. This is learned helplessness, and even in dogs, it is not limited to a single, specific situation or location, such as an experimental shuttle box.

When they were placed in different experiments involving different adverse conditions, the dogs who had learned they were helpless continued to behave as though they had no control over their experiences. Whenever various negative things came their way, they stayed there and suffered.

Human beings have more complex, highly developed mental skills, of course. Yet Seligman and his colleagues found similar results when they exposed people to unpleasant stimuli. In those experiments, human subjects were exposed not to electric shock, but to loud noise. Some people were placed in the "escapable noise" condition. They could shut off the noise by pressing a button on a panel in front of them, and they reliably did so. Others, in the "inescapable noise" condition, initially tried pressing the button but found nothing happened. In later sessions, they didn't even try, even though the button would have worked. Like the dogs, they quickly learned to believe they were helpless, even though they were not.

Critics of applying these findings to human depression say human beings in real-life situations have to cope with problems that are much more nuanced than making simple choices in controlled lab experiments. Furthermore, the interaction between our thoughts, our emotions, and our environments is unbelievably complicated. They say depression cannot be boiled down to something as simple as learned helplessness.

I am sure those critics are at least partially right in some cases. But I also know my own experience, and my experience often felt a lot like inescapable noise and shock. In the real world, we call it being trapped in a dead-end job, or being stuck in a relationship, or putting up with physical or emotional abuse. We believe there are unavoidable or inescapable situations we are powerless to change. It is the belief in our inability to cope or to change things that keeps us from trying, even when, unbeknownst to us, the circumstances may have changed. This even includes circumstances inside us, such as the acquisition of new skills and knowledge and achieving new levels of maturity.

What does unavoidable stress feel like in your life? Is it a chronic or life-threatening illness? Is it a marriage that feels empty and pointless? Is it a situation with your children who keep creating problems for themselves and for you by their poor choices? Is it an addiction you feel you can't overcome? Is it a set of ongoing financial problems? Is it a job where you feel you'll never catch up on your backlog of work or be recognized for your achievements? Ask yourself: Are there parts of your life where you feel you have no control over what happens to you?

Then ask how you respond to unavoidable stress. Have you given up trying to control a certain part of your environment? Do you believe you don't have any choices? Are you just lying down and taking it? Does it feel pointless to even try, because you know whatever you do isn't going to make a difference? I'm going to repeat the question, because I really want you to hear it.

Does it feel pointless to even try, because you know whatever you do isn't going to make a difference? If it does, then you may well be a normal person living in circumstances that make you feel depressed—just as my counselor, Jim, told me all those years ago.

Whether you feel deeply depressed or mildly so, you

can change the way you feel by changing the way you think. If you think you have a depressive personality, you can change the way you feel by changing the way you think. If you are reasonably happy but would like more out of life, you can change the way you feel by changing the way you think.

By changing the way you think, you can change the products of your thoughts, which are your feelings and your beliefs. False beliefs about yourself, about others, and about the world in general lie at the root of so many seemingly intractable problems. When I coach someone, every time, without fail, there comes a moment where a connection is made and the light goes on. I know it at the moment it happens, because the person's face is transformed. I can literally see the "Aha!" moment. I know things will be different for the person from that moment forward, the same way things were different for me after the moment in Jim's office.

The moment of realization is not a cure for depression. It is not an epiphany that solves everything. It is the rebirth of hope after hope has been lost. The moment when I see hope blooming in the face of another person, it is reborn in me, and we are both stronger for it. The rest of this book is my attempt to give you the same hope, to ensure hope's survival and growth, and to help you find the stunning results hope can produce.

Continuing the Journey
Questions and actions for moving forward

- Notice when you use *should* statements. What are they, and what are you trying to achieve by using them?
- Notice your responses to everyday events, such as inclement weather, difficult traffic conditions, or an unpleasant interaction with a family member. What story did you create about the event and its meaning? What conclusions did you come to?
- If negative feelings persist after an event ends, examine what you are saying to yourself about what happened. What meanings did you assign? What judgments did you make?
- Are there situations in your life where you feel you have no choice? Is that opinion objectively true? Are you willing to try to create a difference by making a small change?
- To improve your mood, deliberately practice the creation of positive emotion by reliving good memories. Focus on the feelings you had at the time, and you can re-experience them.

— Chapter 5 —

The Most Convincing Storyteller

After the end of each year, I go through the files which have accumulated in my office. I sort and purge, set aside the records I need for income taxes, and start new files for the new year. A few years ago, a friend was helping me with this process, which included going through a basket of papers that had not been filed yet. Among those papers was a two-page print-out of instructions for printing an envelope in my laser printer, something I only need to do about four times a year.

I wasn't sure where to put it so I could find it the next time I needed it. I didn't want to have to search online for the obscure directions in three months. I ask myself a standard question when I'm trying to find a place to store objects in my house: "When I need this again, where will I look for it?" It's amazing how well it works, but the only answer I could come up with was a file folder labeled "Printer." My friend suggested I make such a file and put the two sheets of paper in it, but I resisted. It was the obvious solution, but I hadn't let myself consider it. In my mind, files were for broad categories of items, like bank statements or car maintenance records. Two sheets of paper were not enough to justify a dedicated file.

This was the height of silliness. What did I think? The file police were going to burst through the door and demand to inspect my system? What is the penalty for having fewer than ten sheets of paper in a file, anyway? In my case, the self-imposed penalty was a basket of disorganized papers cluttering up my workspace because I refused to create a sensible place to put them.

Sometimes the answer to a problem is so easy we can't see it. It is in a blind spot created by our unconscious beliefs. I thought there was an official way, or at least a right way, to keep files. I want to do things the right way. It wasn't until my friend questioned my belief that I realized what was probably obvious to the rest of the world. The purpose of my filing system is to serve me, not to meet some external standard. Today, I have more files than ever, and my workspace is much less cluttered.

I had concocted a story about how my home office should be set up. The story's ingredients were thoughts I had collected over time. I included things I learned in school, such as how to alphabetize and categorize; things I learned in my family, such as the importance of being a good girl and doing things perfectly whenever possible; and things I learned casually, just from living, such as how unpleasant an audit from the IRS can be if you have not kept meticulous files.

I did not set out to create a story or a set of beliefs about filing systems. I was not even aware I was creating the story, much less being deliberate about it. I didn't even know I had such a story until my friend questioned why I didn't just go for the simple answer to the problem of the printer instructions.

I have a massive collection of stories about how the world works, how things should be, what is possible and what is not. I have many stories about what I am like, how I should be, what I can and cannot do. And I have stories about what other people are like, how they should be, and what kinds of relationships are possible. You have a massive collection of stories, too. Although you probably have had many collaborators over the years, you are ultimately the author of every single one of them. Based on your experiences, your thoughts, and your beliefs, you assume all your stories are true. You are the most convincing storyteller ever. You make up stories and then you live them out—which makes them come true for you. All you have to do to verify the truth of your stories is to look at your actions, which are based on your stories. Through this circular process, beliefs are reinforced until we think they are the Truth with a capital T.

You believe the things you say to yourself. You wouldn't knowingly lie to yourself, because you know when you are lying. (This is one of the reasons I don't recommend straight-up positive thinking to create change.) The problem with some of our stories is that they are not completely true, even when they are not outright lies. Yet we believe them anyway. Our faith in our own stories often leads us to make mistakes, make poor choices, and create negative moods for ourselves to live in.

Everyone has his or her own patterns of storytelling, developed over a lifetime. Our brains create stories in order to make sense of the world and explain things. If I know the story of gravity, I don't have to guess whether the ball I toss into the air will come back down or float away. If I understand that rain only comes when there are clouds in the sky, I can prepare by taking an umbrella on an overcast day. Seeing the world as predictable helps us to feel secure. We need our stories to make sense of things. These kinds of explanations are obvious, but we go farther and deeper, attempting to explain things which may not be explainable. Our most emotionally important stories are the ones which assign value to ourselves and others and meaning to events.

It begins when we are toddlers, if not earlier. We learn what it means to be a good or bad girl or boy. In school, we learn what it means to be a good or bad student. In the family, we learn what it means to be of a certain ethnicity or religion. Everywhere we go, we collect information that we assemble into stories to explain who and what we are and how we got to be that way. We create stories about everything we see and every circumstance we encounter, but we don't call the results of this process stories. We call it the way things are. We call it reality. We call it the Truth.

Knowing the way things are is vital for coping in a complex and changing world. If you know what it takes to please your parents, or how to attract a desirable mate, or how to earn a good living, your life will be much more pleasant and less painful. But what happens when you are doing the best you can, but your parents aren't pleased, or the person you have a crush on doesn't know or care you are alive, or you find yourself in a job where you just can't get ahead? The stories you tell yourself in challenging or disappointing situations determine how well you will cope in the moment, recover from setbacks, and move forward.

One critical question is involved in creating explanations of what happens to you. How you answer this question will determine how you see yourself, how you see others, and how you see the entire world. The question is a single word: why.

We learn the word why nearly as soon as we begin to speak, and if you are a parent, you know it can be the single most annoying word in the world. Young children go through a phase of asking why about everything. Why is the sky blue? Why do I have to take a nap? Why can birds fly? Why can't I have ice cream for breakfast? Why does glass break? The questions are endless during this stage of life, because children are trying to make sense of so many things. They are constantly looking for explanations, and many an exasperated parent has resorted to the ultimate answer when asked such questions as, "Why do I have to take a bath?" The ultimate answer, of course, is "Because I said so!"

We continue to ask why questions all through our lives, but we internalize them as we grow older and more mature. We think we should be able to figure things out, and we usually do come up with explanations. The quality of those explanations varies widely. One reason for this variety is called explanatory style.

When we are learning to explain things, we tend to settle into attitudes that create predictable patterns in our stories. Martin Seligman identified three aspects of explanatory style that tend to solidify into habits over time. He calls them the three Ps: permanence, pervasiveness, and personalization. How you handle these three aspects of explanation can determine how you feel about virtually everything that happens to you.

Permanence defines how long-lasting you believe circumstances to be. Is it a momentary blip or the way of the world? Is whatever caused the event you are explaining temporary or permanent? If you see bad things as permanent, but believe good things are only temporary, your style is more pessimistic. You will say things like, "I have no talent for golf," and "I just got lucky with that shot." A more optimistic style is to see good things as permanent and bad things as temporary. In that case, you would say, "I've always had a knack for baking," and "I burned the brownies because I forgot to set the timer."

Pervasiveness in explanations deals with how much you believe your life or the world at large is affected by what has happened. How much ground does your explanation cover? Negative explanations of bad events tend toward the overall attitude of, "I'm a loser," or "Things never go my way." Negative explanations of good events tend to be more limited, such as, "I was just in the right place at the right time, for once in my life." Meanwhile, putting a positive spin on bad events means you see them as narrower in scope, as in, "My husband is grouchy because he got a speeding ticket." Positive explanations of good things tend to paint them as universal, such as, "People are generally good at heart."

Personalization has to do with the position in which you place yourself in the explanation. Were you in control of the situation or not? Were you to blame if things went badly? Did you take the credit if things went well? Seligman says there are two approaches to personalization, external and internal. In external personalization, someone or something else is either to blame or deserves the credit. In the external personalization style, you don't take responsibility for whatever happened, whether the event was negative or positive. Examples of external personalization include, in a positive slant, "The traffic made me late." On the negative side, you might say, "It was just dumb luck that I won the concert tickets." The reverse is true in internal personalization. Using the same two situations above, you could say, negatively, "I'm a chronically tardy person," and positively, "I won the concert tickets because I am good at trivia games."

In external explanations, when something good happens, you give yourself no credit, and when something bad happens, you don't blame yourself. In internal explanations, when something good happens, you claim credit, and when it's something bad, you take the blame. Seligman says pessimists tend not to take credit but to blame themselves, while optimists take credit and blame others or circumstances. Not surprisingly, pessimists are much more likely to become depressed.

Explanatory style is not the only element of self-talk, but it may be the factor you are least familiar with. When trying to determine your style, it may help to write down your thoughts about a given situation, and then go back and analyze them.

As I was working on this section of the book, I found myself continually distracted by the beautiful weather outside. I decided to carry my laptop out to the balcony of my rented condo overlooking the Gulf of Mexico. I wanted to enjoy the sunshine and the sound of the waves while getting some work done. I found myself just sitting for stretches of time, basking in the warmth of the sun, and thinking how grateful I was to be out of the cold weather back home, where five inches of snow covered the ground. I daydreamed about what life would be like if I could spend the coldest months of every winter in a place like this. I could walk on the beach every day, eat great seafood, and spend time with friends. It was a lovely picture and I was loath to leave it. But I reminded myself that this Florida retreat was specifically for the purpose of writing this book. I was determined to go home with a completed first draft.

I picked up my computer and went back inside, saying to myself, "Stop being so lazy! You are never going to get this book done at the rate you are going. You have the attention span of a gnat. What would your mastermind group say if they knew how much time you're spending goofing off? Goofing off is one of the things you are best at, isn't it? You pretty much make a career of it. Too bad you can't get paid for it. You'd be a billionaire!"

Allow me to introduce you to someone I know intimately well: Little Miss Goody Two Shoes, my inner critic. She is always on the job, hyper-vigilant, ready to offer a quick and cutting criticism any time she perceives I am doing something wrong. Even when I am doing something good and right, she is there, telling me I should be doing it better or faster, or offering the opinion that this chunk of time might be better used to do something different. For example, as I dutifully sit indoors, typing away on my manuscript, she whispers about how I should have managed my time and energy better so I could go out for a walk this afternoon. After all, she says, I am already too fat, and I am not getting any skinnier sitting here munching on pistachios as I work. If only I weren't so lazy, I could have worked harder over the previous few days and had time for a walk.

Little Miss Goody Two Shoes, or Goody for short, knows a thing or two about storytelling, and she is a pessimistic little monster. Let's look at the three Ps in her take on my struggle with temptation.

Is it pervasive? Yes, if I've made a career of goofing off. Is it personal? The label of lazy is most definitely personal, and so is saying my attention span is too short. Is it permanent? Apparently so, as the book is never going to be done. In my self-criticism, I blame myself for failing, a permanent assessment, and I say this is happening because of my own shortcomings.

And yet, you are reading the book. Somehow, it did get finished.

Your explanatory style is habitual, but even strong habits can be broken, weakened, or replaced. If the habit of negativity is deeply ingrained, you may sometimes default to a pessimistic style, even after you have learned a different way. However, you do not have to stick with the first story you tell yourself, which may be the one your inner critic is creating. Learning to listen to your stories, ask questions about them, and be willing to rewrite them is a strategy that can turn pessimists into optimists, cynics into dreamers, and depressed people into happy people. This skill can change your life. I know, because it changed mine.

When I was depressed, I thought I didn't have the right to please myself, especially if it meant someone else might get less than everything they wanted. I started to come out of the depression when I began to ask myself what I liked to do or to have or to be. Then I began to honor myself the same way I honored others. It felt freakishly strange at first.

Let's delve into this idea of pleasing yourself a little further.

Wait, do you hear something? Are alarm bells going off in your head? You may have a little mental gremlin like Goody. Whenever I think of pleasing myself instead of putting others first, she presses the alarm button and starts shrieking. She sounds like this: You are so selfish! You are so self-centered! What a nasty little narcissist! What about your children, your friends, your parents, those starving children everywhere in the world? How dare you? You are bad! You are evil! You are going straight to Hell for even thinking this way! You're so bad that when you get to Hell, you are going to be in the express lane!

As I said, she is a wicked little force to be reckoned with, and she has an inordinate love for exclamation points. If you have an inner critic like her, you need a plan in place, or you're never going to have very much fun.

My permanent plan is to remind Little Miss Goody Two Shoes that I am not much help to anyone else if my energy reserves are empty. If I am going to give to others, whether I'm giving time, energy, information, or money, I have to first meet my own needs for nourishment. I can't serve my family, my friends, or you, dear reader, if I am dropping in my tracks from exhaustion. I can't teach others how to be happier if I am allowing myself to sink into depressed thinking. I know I cannot give out of an empty pocket. Therefore, it must not be selfish to take care of my own happiness first. We can give by making sacrifices, but by definition, sacrifice hurts. On the other hand, giving out of abundance is a blessing, to you as well as to the receiver. You may have been sold, as I was, on the idea that sacrificing for others is the best, purest kind of giving. Giving all you have may be the ideal in spiritual theory, but in reality, it is not only unsustainable, but impossible.

Remind your inner critic that you must take care of your own needs if you are to help others. Then, stick by your decision, even if it means you have to reason with your critic multiple times a day. Little Miss Goody Two Shoes still lives in my head, and she probably always will, but she is much quieter than she used to be. You can also quiet your inner critic and begin to change your beliefs for the better. When you do, you will begin to feel less depressed and start growing happiness for yourself and those around you.

Continuing the Journey
Questions and actions for moving forward

- When something you consider to be negative happens, write down your explanation of why it happened the way it did. Then, examine your explanation for words describing permanence, pervasiveness, and personalization. This can help you identify your explanatory style.
- Do the same thing when something happens that you consider to be positive.
- Listen to your inner critic when he or she starts finding fault with you. Write down some of the statements the inner critic makes and determine how much truth they hold. Look for words that indicate permanence, pervasiveness, and personalization.
- Give your inner critic a fitting name. Doing this really will make it easier to talk back to him or her when necessary.

— Chapter 6 —

From Wet Blanket to Warm Fuzzy

The crucial first step that set my far-reaching changes in motion was seeing myself in a different light. This is sometimes called a "paradigm shift," an unfortunately dense term that simply means you see things in a way you have not seen them before. Your ideas and beliefs change radically.

When your paradigm shifts, an internal process occurs. Nothing in the external world changes. This is why I end every A Decided Difference podcast with the words, "The world doesn't change. You do." If you are standing at the bottom of a mountain, you see things from the bottom-of-the-mountain perspective. When you climb to the top, the scenery hasn't changed. The trees and streams and rocks are still in the same places, but everything looks quite different when you see it from the top-of-the-mountain perspective.

When I began to see myself as a normal person

coping with difficult circumstances, nothing about those circumstances changed, at least not at first. What changed was the way I looked at the circumstances and how I thought about them. Then I began to gather ideas of what I could do about all of it. When my inner world changed, my outer world changed, too. This wasn't because of my thinking alone, but because of the actions I took based on my different thinking. This process absolutely works for both better and worse. Your thoughts have a powerful influence on your external world.

Scientists theorize humans are the only creatures who are capable of thinking about their own thoughts, but you probably have never been taught ways to think most effectively. As I said in Chapter 2, thinking is a skill, and that means it can be learned and developed. Just as a golfer can improve her performance by learning and then practicing a better swing, you can improve your performance by learning and practicing better ways to think. Learning to think consciously and deliberately can change your life, and that change can begin right away.

You already know how to do everything I am going to recommend. You don't have to learn any new skills, but you do have to learn to apply what you know in different ways. I am going to ask you to listen, to ask questions, to think of alternatives, and to tell stories. You already do this, every day, all day long. The golfer in my example already knows how to play the game, but she can take strokes off her score when she learns a better way to hold the club. Naturally, this takes practice. So does learning a different way to hold your thoughts.

Our minds are busy all the time. I wanted to insert an

impressive statistic here, telling you how many thoughts the average person has in a day, but I couldn't find a reliable source for that information. The estimates I found ranged from three per minute up to 100,000 per day. I'm not sure it's even possible to count such a thing. Let's just say you think all the time, mostly without conscious awareness of what is driving the thoughts.

You can't choose to change what you don't know about. Awareness is the first key step in making any kind of change. How long has it been since you consciously tuned in to what you are saying in your running inner conversation? I call it your mental soundtrack, because it plays in the background all the time. Let's take a few moments to look at what kinds of thoughts are filling your mind, day in and day out.

We frequently have observational thoughts like these: We are running low on toothpaste. This sandwich is better than the one I had yesterday. That's a cute pair of jeans she is wearing. There is dog hair on the sofa. These thoughts don't involve much emotion, and many of them are trivial. You have hundreds, if not thousands, of thoughts like these in a day.

Other thoughts are somewhat important as you go through each day, such as: How much money is left in the checking account? Do we have enough eggs for breakfast tomorrow? The car needs its oil changed. I need to talk to Mary before the meeting this afternoon. I call these operational thoughts. They have to do with your activities, planning, and functioning in the setting of daily life.

Then there are aspirational thoughts—thoughts that have to do with improving yourself or your situation, hopes, dreams, and plans. These are thoughts such as, I want to go to the beach on vacation this year. I want a promotion and the raise that goes with it. I want my children to grow up happy and strong. I want to take a class and learn something new. When we get into the aspirational realm, we start to venture into storytelling, albeit in the future tense. We think of things we believe will make our lives better or more meaningful.

Moving further into storytelling, we also have daydream thoughts: I wish I could paint like Virginia does. If I won the lottery, I would never have to worry about money again. I wish my boss would move to Timbuktu. If I could just meet the right person for me, I would be happy. Daydream thoughts often include the word "wish" or the phrase, "If only." These thoughts can give you a little escape from the stresses in your life. They are harmless as long as you keep them in perspective. It's one thing to daydream about the beach house you would buy if you won the Mega Millions; it is something else altogether to spend a hundred dollars a week on lottery tickets.

When we venture into explanatory thoughts, we are into pure storytelling. In explanatory thoughts, you explain why things happen and what it means to you and about you. I want to be very clear about this. We can easily tell ourselves stories which are not true and/or stories that do not serve us well. But because they are our own stories, we believe them.

The problem with explanatory thoughts is that you can't always explain things. You may not know why something happened the way it did. You may never be able to know all the reasons why, but your mind does not like open loops. The human brain craves closure, and if getting it means you have to make up a plausible story to fill in the gaps, you will do it. You are not necessarily conscious of doing this. In fact, it's highly likely you are not aware of it.

The thoughts that cause us the most trouble are the thoughts where we negatively judge ourselves and others. If you are reading this because you are interested in positive change, the chances are excellent that you sometimes, if not frequently, judge yourself too harshly. It is easy to fall into the habit of throwing a wet blanket on your own hopes.

When you tell yourself judgmental stories, you often assign meanings that describe who you are, rather than simply what you did. Let's say you made a mathematical error in your checking account, and you thought you had more money than you did. You went out and bought something new or splurged on a treat, only to realize too late you did not actually have the money in your budget. What do you say to yourself in this situation? Do you say things like this? I am such an idiot. Why do I always mess things up? I've never been any good at math, and it will always cause me problems. I don't know what I was thinking. I should have known better. My spouse is going to hate me.

What if you interviewed for a new job, and in your opinion, it didn't go very well? You drew a blank when the interviewer asked you an important question. You nervously stammered even when you knew the answers. Her body language said she was not impressed with you at all. The interview ended with her saying something vague about how they would try to get back with you in a week or two. What do you tell yourself on your way home? Well, I completely blew that. I looked like a total fool in there. She must have thought I was stupid, and she obviously couldn't wait to get out of there. I am never going to hear from them.

If these sound like the kinds of things you say to yourself when things go wrong, there is a simple but important step to help you feel better right away. Build awareness of your own mental soundtrack by writing down the thoughts you have when things don't go your way. Seriously, write them down—don't just think about them. This can give you a bit of perspective that is hard to see otherwise. Then, when you get them down on paper, look for patterns of thinking which lead you to feel bad about yourself. By the way, I'm not just interested in helping you feel better, although I firmly believe that is a worthy thing. I want you to do better, to be able to take better actions. If you have bad feelings toward yourself, it can cause you to take self-defeating actions, and those actions can make things worse for real.

When you get your thoughts written down, examine them for these and similar words:

- Always
- Ever
- Completely
- Totally
- Constantly
- No way
- Not ever
- Never

These all-or-nothing words are very seldom true—but I won't say never. Let's look at our examples:

- Why do I *always* mess things up?
- I've *never* been any good at math, and it will *always* cause me problems.
- I *completely* blew that.
- I looked like a *total* fool in there.
- I am *never* going to hear from them.

Objectively, you do not always mess things up, and no one is a total fool. But when you choose these words for your stories, you make yourself feel as though things will never get better, and you will always have problems. If that were true, your situation would be hopeless, and feeling hopeless leads to feelings of discouragement and depression. You don't want to go there.

Another mistake we make in our stories is reading the minds and predicting the actions of other people. My spouse is going to hate me. She must have thought I was stupid, and she obviously couldn't wait to get out of there. I am never going to hear from them.

If your spouse hates you for one mistake, you might have married the wrong person. You can't know if the interviewer thought you were stupid. Even if it were true she couldn't wait to leave, you have no idea why. Is it possible her babysitter called to say her child was sick, or she had to get to the bank before it closed, or she really, really had to use the restroom?

We can make all kinds of errors in our stories, but because we think we know exactly what happened, we believe our own explanations. I love seeing the bumper stickers that say, "Don't believe everything you think." It is excellent advice.

But let's say the interview really did go badly, and you really are not going to be offered the job. Does it serve you to call yourself a fool? When you look at the thoughts you write down, check to see if you're calling yourself names or labeling yourself with negative words. Would you say those things aloud to a person you cared about?

There is one attitude I want you to shift right away, and it is a simple change to make. It may feel a little weird at first, and it will take repetition to make it a habit, but it is one of the most crucial changes you can make. If you change nothing but this one attitude, you will be happier: Immediately start treating yourself with kindness.

Think of the person in the world you are closest to. It could be a spouse, a child, a parent, a friend. Think about how much you love this person. Think about how you feel when you are together. Think about how you share confidences or how you laugh together. Think of all the dimension this person brings to your life, and how lost you would feel without him or her. Feel gratitude for the love you have for this person, and the love he or she has for you. Really do this, right now. Bask in the good feelings for as long as you like.

Now, imagine that the next time this beloved person walks into your living room, you speak to him or her the same way you speak to yourself. Would you say, "Hey there, loser! I'm so glad you could finally show up. If you weren't so lazy and rude, you would have been here half an hour earlier. Speaking of lazy, have you gained another five pounds on top of the extra weight you were already carrying? You know you should cut out all those sweets, not to mention the fast food. If you'd take your lard butt out for a walk every now and then, maybe you wouldn't look so disgusting."

I could go on, but you get the picture. You would not dream of speaking to your best friend—or even a stranger—this way, so why in the world is it all right to do it when you talk to yourself? It isn't all right. It's hurtful, and we have enough hurt in this world.

In workshops, I sometimes ask participants to write down some of the things they say to themselves during the course of a normal day. Then, I instruct them to turn to the person seated next to them and say those things aloud to that person. They are mortified at the mere thought of doing it. Yet they say those things to themselves on a regular basis.

As I was reading through a draft of this chapter, a friend walked into the room. Without looking up from the page, I started reading the negative self-talk paragraph above. Out loud. To him.

"Hey there, loser! I'm so glad you could finally show up. If you weren't so lazy and rude, you would have been here half an hour earlier. Speaking of lazy, have you gained another five pounds . . ." When I looked up, he was standing frozen, a stricken look on his face. I told him what I was doing, saying out loud to him the things I say to myself. He was relieved, obviously, but he also said something quite telling.

"Those things are probably true about me, but I didn't

know why you were being so mean about it." He said he believed some of those things about himself and immediately started beating himself up. This process is important to understand, and the seriousness of it is important to recognize. This kind of negative self-talk affects all of us, no matter how optimistic we may naturally be. We are all susceptible to its damaging effects.

Look, I get it. I know why you are talking differently to yourself than to your friends and family members. You are trying to motivate yourself to be a better person. You want to be a healthy, attractive, industrious, intelligent, polite person, so you call yourself fat, gross, ugly, lazy, and stupid, hoping it will spur you to change. Should work, right? Has it worked so far? (Did you catch the use of the S-word just now?)

If you were trying to help a person you love to make changes, would you do it by insulting, shaming, and name calling? Why not?

We beat ourselves up because we know we are capable of being better. I do this, too, although I certainly do it a lot less than I used to. When I catch myself doing it, I am pretty good at hauling myself up short and taking a different approach. I have learned to tell Little Miss Goody Two Shoes to quiet down or to point out the lies she tells me.

Beating yourself up does not make you a better person. It makes you a beaten person. You don't deserve that, and it isn't working anyway. Plus, it's making you feel terrible. So get ready to try something different. You don't have to be mean to yourself to improve yourself or to change things in your life. Having compassion for yourself and practicing self-forgiveness can be very freeing, and feeling free to change is an essential step in making change. You are the person closest to you. You are the person at the center of your life. You deserve to be treated with kindness, acceptance, and compassion. I don't deserve to hear the things Goody says to me, and you don't deserve to hear the things your internal critic says to you.

Try being kinder to yourself and see if your mood doesn't immediately get better. When it does, you may actually have the energy to make your situation better, too.

Accepting others as they are is a foundation of friendship and caring. If there are things about yourself you want to change, you may find self-acceptance difficult, but it is also the foundation of caring for yourself. Decide to be nice to yourself, to hold compassion for yourself, and to encourage yourself.

You may be thinking, wait a minute. Are you saying I should let myself off the hook every single time I mess up?

That depends on what you mean by off the hook. When things don't turn out the way you would like, there is nothing wrong with asking why or making plans to do better the next time. What I argue against is the self-condemnation that often goes along with it. If you make a mistake, you are not stupid. If you fail at something, you are not a loser. No matter how hard you try, things will not always go the way you would like. Learning from experience is how we all grow. You don't have to be judgmental, hateful, or insulting toward yourself to get the lesson.

Sam Walton, one of the most successful businessmen of all time, gave advice about running a thriving company in his autobiography, Made In America. He wrote, "Nothing else can quite substitute for a few well-chosen, well-timed, sincere words of praise. They're absolutely free—and worth a fortune." He was suggesting saying those words of praise to employees, but I think saying them to yourself is just as important. Praising yourself when you do well may feel awkward and egotistical at first, but praise that is sincere is very motivating, even if it comes from yourself.

Imagine saying these things to yourself and notice how you feel.

- You did a good job.
- That's the way to hang in there!
- You look very nice today.
- You knocked them out with your presentation.
- I'm proud of you.
- You cooked a delicious meal.
- You are getting better and better at this.

You can probably very easily imagine saying those things to a child, an employee, a friend, or anyone else you want to encourage, because you know it will help them. There is nothing wrong with saying the same things to help yourself. On the contrary, there is everything right about encouraging yourself if you want to make genuine improvement.

Continuing the Journey
Questions and actions for moving forward

- Really write down the thoughts you have when things don't go your way. I mean it—really do it. Get it out of your head and on paper where you can see it. Really! (Is that too many uses of "really"? Goody thinks it is.)
- Look at what you have written and ask yourself if the statements are objectively true, or if you are engaging in reading the minds of others, or if you are beating yourself up.
- Imagine saying the things you have written out loud to someone you love. If you wouldn't do it to them, don't do it to yourself.
- Decide to be kind to yourself.
- Find fresh encouragement weekly in my podcast, *A Decided Difference.* You can find all available episodes here: http://decideddifference.libsyn.com/. You can also subscribe wherever you get your pod-casts to receive a new episode each Monday morning.

— Chapter 7 —

Spotlight on Happiness

The human brain has amazing capabilities to fool itself. From optical illusions to delusional thoughts, the brain and its systems are busy creating your experience of reality 24 hours a day, every day of your life. In the last chapter, I talked about many of the ways your brain presents you with a distorted version of reality. The stories your brain makes up not only are distorted, they also skew to the negative. The human brain is said to have a negativity bias. When presented with all the information it must process in the course of a day, your brain automatically and predictably pays more attention to information about what is ugly, risky, and dangerous. When others speak to you, your brain will highlight anything they say that is critical, threatening, or nasty in any way. Your brain is exquisitely sensitive to the facial expressions of other people and will notice frowns, smirks, and grimaces, even if they last only a fraction of a second.

The commonly accepted theory is that modern humans evolved to be more sensitive to negative information than to positive input, because paying attention to danger is a survival mechanism. Your brain gives priority to threatening information because you carry the genes of your ancestors, the ones who survived despite dangers in the environment. Unfortunately, the brain's inborn tendency to focus on threats keeps it constantly looking for danger, even when we are in safe surroundings. If there are no lions or tigers or bears around, we tend to notice threats of a social nature, such as criticism from another or body language that says someone doesn't want to be near us.

There is another function of the brain that, when combined with our bias toward negativity, contributes to making us feel bad. Your brain will automatically seek, find, and magnify whatever you expect, think about, or focus on. It doesn't matter if you are anticipating something consciously or subconsciously. Whatever is on your mind will appear in your world, because having it on your mind will make you look for it. Paying attention to it will make it seem important, whether it is or not. Your natural tendency is to believe things are more prevalent or meaningful simply because you have paid attention to them.

This a very important concept when it comes to creating positive feelings, happiness, and optimism, because you have the ability to consciously choose what you will give your attention to.

The reticular activating system, or RAS, is the part of your brain that decides what to see. It sorts out the many stimuli that come into your brain every moment of your life. Right now, you are focusing on reading the words on this page and understanding the information they convey, but torrents of other information are being screened out of your awareness by your RAS. You can take deliberate control and override the system at any moment you choose. Go ahead and try it.

Rather than thinking solely about the words you are reading, think about the feel of the book or electronic device you are holding in your hands. Now think about the pressure on parts of your body as you sit in your chair. Now think about the way your feet feel inside your shoes, or if you happen to be barefoot, how your feet feel against the floor, or a blanket, or whatever they are touching. Think about how your clothes feel as they touch your skin. Think about how your stomach feels. Are you hungry, or do you feel satisfied or even overstuffed because you just had a meal? Now, look around the room you are in. The room I currently occupy has furniture, including a desk, a chair, a cabinet, a bookshelf, and a daybed. It has a rug on the wood floor, blinds on the window, and a ceiling fan with a light fixture. There is a lamp on the desk and a stack of papers nearby. There are dozens of items in this room: plants, books, photographs, a radio, another lamp, blankets, pillows, pencils, pens, a letter opener, a box of tissues, a stapler, paper clips, file folders, an hourglass, a crystal ball, baskets, checkbooks, business cards, a telephone, paintings, and more. Furthermore, each of these individual items has many characteristics.

For example, the African violet on my desk would take quite some time to describe in detail. To start, I could say its leaves are fuzzy and thick and of varying shades of green. Its blossoms are pink with yellow centers. It is rooted in a blue-and-green striped pot filled with organic potting soil and resting in a matching saucer. I could mention it was given to me by my good friend Cara, and I fed it with fertilizer spikes last Sunday. I could say it's looking healthier since it has been given some plant food, and I could add that it is due to be watered tomorrow afternoon.

There are so many things in the environment! And this is just considering the items within a few feet of me. Don't get me started on what I can see out the window in front of me.

Did reading the last paragraphs feel tedious to you? Imagine how difficult your life would be if your RAS did not screen out the majority of sensory inputs that come in through your physical senses. If you had to attend to every detail of your world, you would be so overwhelmed you would struggle to do something as simple as feeding yourself.

The effect of the RAS is so powerful that it can screen out things you think are obvious. To demonstrate this effect, researchers Christopher Chabris and Daniel Simons recorded a video in which two teams of people pass basketballs back and forth. One team is dressed in white shirts; the other team is in black shirts. Viewers of the video are instructed to count the number of times the players wearing white pass the ball. If you would like to try the experiment before reading about the astonishing results, watch the video and play along at http://www.youtube.com/watch?v=vJG698U2Mvo. If you want to avoid the spoiler that follows, watch it right now, before you read any further.

Many people who watch the video are so focused on counting the number of passes that they miss a fairly significant event. About twelve seconds into the video, a person dressed in a gorilla suit walks into the center of the action, pauses to pound his chest, and then walks out. Because the viewer's attention is focused on the players wearing white, half of the viewers, including me the first time I watched it, completely miss the gorilla. This happens because the black gorilla costume blends in with the players wearing black, which is the color viewers are actively ignoring. When you watch the video again and look for it, the gorilla is so obvious it's unbelievable to think you missed it. Yet I did. Lest you think that is just because I'm not very bright, so did about half of the Harvard students who participated in the research. Chabris and Simons wrote a book based on this research and other experiments that show how our brains can trick us, even when we are watching closely with our eyes wide open. They called it, appropriately, The Invisible Gorilla. Now that you know about the gorilla trick, try watching another video produced by Daniel Simons called The Monkey Business Illusion. The video is available online at https://www.youtube.com/watch?v=IGQmdoK_ZfY. I am embarrassed to admit it, but he got me again! If you are interested in learning more, check out theinvisiblegorilla.com.

Now that you have witnessed the power of the RAS,

it's time to learn to program it to serve your goals of healthier thinking and more happiness. The best way I know to help you understand how this works is to tell you the story of hunting Easter eggs.

The story of the Easter egg hunt started with an exercise in the book Finding Your Own North Star by Martha Beck. She calls it the synchronicity exercise and says it is designed to help you discover coincidences that are remarkably unlikely. As you discover these coincidences, you ultimately can prove that life is on your side. The synchronicity exercise is also a demonstration of the same concept illustrated by the invisible gorilla—the concept of selective attention. The best way to explain selective attention in lay person's terms is this: You find what you look for.

Beck suggested you think of an object you might encounter in your daily life but which is somewhat unusual. You might choose to look for orange frogs or cars with unusual decorations attached to them or mice wearing hats. Beck said if you wrote down the object of your choosing, you would be very likely to see it over the next few days.

I admit I was a skeptic. I wanted to prove this to myself in a big way or not at all. Because I was doing this experiment three weeks before Christmas, I decided to look for Easter eggs.

A couple of days after I chose the object to look for, I was staying in a hotel with my young daughter. I ordered coffee with breakfast. When the waitress brought the coffee to the table, it was in a thermal carafe, but it was the strangest one I'd ever seen. It was in the shape of an egg.

That got my attention, but I said myself, "I see the egg, but it's not an Easter egg. It's just a plain white egg, so it doesn't count."

A few days later, I went to visit a friend, and I noticed a large basket of marble eggs on a table near the door. These eggs were all different colors, green and pink and black and yellow, but they weren't really Easter eggs. I asked my friend how long those eggs had been in that spot. She said, "I don't know. Several years?" I had been to this friend's house on numerous occasions and had never noticed the basket of eggs until I decided to hunt Easter eggs at Christmastime.

Less than a week later, I was volunteering at a thrift store operated by Habitat for Humanity. A donation came in, packed in large cardboard boxes that were taped shut. It all had to be sorted, and when I opened the first of the boxes, there they were: hundreds of Easter eggs. There were plastic eggs, glass eggs, tiny eggs to decorate a tiny egg tree, bunnies holding eggs, eggs that nested inside each other like those little Russian dolls, and a wreath covered with Easter eggs. I opened another equally large box, and it also was full to bursting with Easter eggs, eggs of every size, color, and description.

The Great Easter Egg Hunt, as I have come to call it, has continued nonstop for several years. Every time I tell the story, I see an Easter egg in the next couple days.

I told this story once to a young woman after she said there were no good, eligible men to be found in the area where she lived. She was discouraged, thinking she was never going to find anyone she wanted to spend time with, much less fall in love with and marry. I told her the story of finding what you expect to find. I said, "If you tell yourself, There's no one out there. I'm not ever going to meet anybody. All the good men are taken, then guess what? That's exactly what you will find, because it's what you've told yourself to look for." Coincidentally, I told her the story at Christmastime, and I also told her I would see an Easter egg soon. She smiled and nodded politely, but I could tell she didn't believe me. Two days later, while checking in at a hospital lab, I spotted an Easter egg, along with a fuzzy yellow chick, under a potted plant behind the desk. I snapped a photo and texted it to the young lady. That was a few years ago, and today she is happily married to a man whose name is (no kidding) Mr. Wright.

What are you telling yourself to look for? If you believe there is no reason to be happy, there won't be. If you believe there is no reason to be optimistic, that there is no meaning to life, that life is just difficult and then we die, then every day of your life, you will see or create evidence to support what you believe. You see what you look for. I often wear an Easter egg pendant on a chain around my neck to remind myself of this truth. If you hunt Easter eggs, you will find Easter eggs. We absolutely see what we look for. I've seen it play out over and over and over again.

By the way, when you stop looking for something, you stop finding it. That may sound like stating the obvious, but it's like the invisible gorilla. I attended an event where everyone was supposed to bring in food to share. Because it was autumn, the theme was fall foods. This made me think of chili and stew and apples and pumpkins. A friend who had heard the story of looking for Easter eggs in my weekly podcast decided to bring some for me to find. They were brightly dyed and tucked into a colorful container that was obviously an Easter basket. They sat squarely in the middle of the food table, but I didn't notice them until he pointed them out. They were directly in front of me, literally right under my nose, but because I wasn't thinking of looking for Easter eggs that day, I did not see them. Like the gorilla, they were invisible, because I was not expecting to see them. My RAS had screened them out. I was looking for and expected to see only fall foods! Even though I experienced it myself, I still can hardly believe it happened.

So what does all this Easter egg hunting have to do with changing your life through changing your thinking? How about everything?

When you start looking for things to feel grateful for, you will find them. When you start looking for reasons to feel happy, or encouraged, or motivated, you will find them. When you decide to ignore negative news stories, and complainers, and critical, gossipy people, you will start to think the world really is a better place. It will be a better place for you, because you have decided to see it that way.

Please understand, I am not advocating ignoring all your problems or the very real problems of the world around you. I am saying if you focus on really seeing the good things that are happening, you will start to feel encouraged and motivated to pitch in and make things even better, for yourself and those around you. Your hope and your energy will return, and you can build real happiness on a foundation of optimism rooted in reality.

You now understand the operation of your internal dialogue, the endless mental soundtrack. You know how your need to explain events keeps you creating stories about what happens to you. You know how the RAS works to modify your perception of reality. Now, it is time to take the controls and put your brain to work at creating a better mental environment for yourself. It is time to live happily ever after.

Continuing the Journey
Questions and actions for moving forward

- Demonstrate the power of the RAS to yourself by viewing the video at http://www.youtube.com/watch?v=vJG698U2Mvo.
- Try it again with this video: https://www.youtube.com/watch?v=IGQmdoK_ZfY
- Conduct the "synchronicity exercise" for yourself and discover that you do find what you look for.
- Start looking for things to be grateful for, happy about, or encouraged by. Make a note when you see them. Look for more. Feel happier right away.

— Chapter 8 —

Clearing the Mental Clutter

When you decide to see yourself with compassion and treat yourself with kindness, you may feel better immediately. Since it is incredibly unpleasant to be judged and found lacking, all the livelong day, for the great majority of your life, you may find great relief. Conversely, you may feel a little worse once you realize you have been beating yourself up unfairly all these years. You may be angry with yourself. If this happens, laugh and say to yourself, *Oh, look! I'm doing it again!*

Habits are notoriously hard to break, and habits that have been grooved in over years or even decades are extremely hard to break. That's why I recommend you don't try to break them at all. Instead, I suggest you practice noticing when you engage in a habit you no longer want. Then, immediately replace it with a different behavior you know will serve you better. I don't think you break old habits as much as you build new ones to crowd them out.

Patterns of thinking you have engaged in for years happen so automatically that you are not aware of them as they run in the background of your mind. They are just part of the scenery, like the sky. That is why the next step in the Decided Difference process is to allow yourself to question everything—and I do mean everything. It is all right to question your assumptions, your ideas, your beliefs about what is possible, and the things you believe are non-negotiable. These can be thoughts about such things as what it takes to be a good person, how you determine right and wrong, and what it means to be selfish. The stuff going on in your head all this time has left you tired, discouraged, anxious, stuck, fearful, or even depressed. There are some good thoughts in there, too, but your mind is like an overstuffed closet that needs to be decluttered. If you clear out the old, ratty sweaters, the pants that no longer fit, and the shoes you never wear because they hurt your feet, you will be left with the clothes that suit you and make you feel good. Furthermore, you will make room to bring in a bunch of flattering clothes that do fit you, as well as shiny new shoes that are cute and comfy.

When you clear out your mind, the first step is much the same as clearing out a closet. You have to take things out and look at them before deciding whether they go back in or get tossed in the trash. With clothes, the only ones you want to keep are the ones that still fit, don't have holes or stains, and you still like. Many of us carry around outdated beliefs we learned in childhood, even though they no longer fit us. Many of our ways of thinking have holes in them or are stained by negative experiences in years past. Once you have discarded the thoughts that no longer serve you (assuming they ever did!), you will have plenty of room to acquire new thoughts to make you happier, healthier, and more successful.

Decluttering thoughts is not exactly like clearing a closet, however. When you throw out an old pair of jeans, they don't try to sneak back in when you aren't looking. Not only will you need to create new thoughts to fill your mind, you will need to put up barriers to keep the old ones from taking over again.

We have already covered judging yourself too harshly. Let's take a look at other old thoughts, beliefs, and actions you may want to get rid of. These include:

- Magnifying the negative
- Minimizing the positive
- Feeling inappropriate guilt
- Giving too much weight to the opinions of others
- Comparing yourself to others
- Assuming there are only two choices in any given situation
- Making negative predictions about the future
- Taking things personally when they are not personal
- Pleasing others but not pleasing yourself
- Ignoring your physical body
- Feeling unworthy

- Thinking you "should" do, be, or think certain ways
- Overestimating dangers
- Not trusting your own judgment
- Sleepwalking through life
- Accepting negative thoughts without questioning them
- Taking responsibility for things that are not within your control
- Choosing discouraging language
- Believing failure is always negative
- Thinking small changes are not worthwhile
- Believing in fate or destiny
- Waiting until the time is right or until you deserve to be happy
- Believing it is selfish to want to be happy

You may discover items to add to the list once you start the process of clearing out your mental closet. This is a deeply personal process, and although an item may not be on my list, it may very well belong on yours.

Let's consider each of these habits of thought and whether they are worth keeping.

Magnifying the negative
A friend's young daughter was playing at my house one afternoon when she discovered a magnifying glass in my desk drawer. Fascinated, she went all around the house, peering through the glass at one item after another. She came skipping into my office and announced, "Your dog has a really big nose!"

It's easy to laugh at the viewpoint of a six-year-old thinking a magnifying glass changes the actual size of things—until you realize how easily your mind does the same thing. How risky do you think it is to fly? How likely is it that you or someone you know will be the victim of a terrorist attack or a mass shooting? How dangerous are food additives, or air pollution, or roller skates? You may believe these things are far riskier than they actually are, especially if you keep up with the news. The human brain has a tendency to believe things are larger, more prevalent, or more dangerous, simply because you have paid attention to them.

This mental trick can be turned to your advantage if you use it consciously. You can choose to look for things that make you feel happy, or justifications for having faith in the human race, or reasons for optimism and hope. You can also choose to look for things that bring joy, simply because they are beautiful to the eye or the ear.

Minimizing the positive

This is the exact opposite of the trick above. When something good happens or you receive encouraging news, do you minimize it by saying it doesn't matter or it doesn't make enough of a difference? Do you think the good thing is too little, or too late, or too much, or too soon? In other words, do you find fault with everything that happens, no matter how wonderful it appears on the surface? My maternal grandmother was one of the most pessimistic people I ever knew, and this was one of her favorite mental magic tricks. If she saw a flash of silver, she would immediately look for the cloud, and she usually found it. This is the technique we employ to deflect compliments. If someone gives you a compliment and you brush it off in a misguided effort to be modest, you are minimizing the positive. Choosing to accept compliments is one of the easiest ways to change your thinking to a more positive slant. Remind yourself that it is pleasant to pay a compliment, just as giving a gift is pleasant. You deprive the giver of his or her joy when you reject the gift of praise.

Like magnifying the negative, this technique can be put to work for you by flipping it around. Rather than minimizing positive things, try minimizing the amount of attention you give to negatives. If you do nothing but reverse these two bad habits, your mood is likely to be vastly improved.

Feeling inappropriate guilt

Feeling guilt can be a useful emotion, if and when you have done something you regret. Knowing you hurt someone else by your words, your actions, or your lack of action can produce feelings of guilt, which serve a purpose. Guilt is an unpleasant emotion, one that can motivate you to avoid doing things that bring it on. I am all for guilt when it is deserved. In fact, I can think of some people who definitely could stand to feel it more often. Unfortunately, it sometimes seems the people who feel the most guilt are the ones who deserve it the least.

Feeling guilt is useful for only one thing: changing future behavior. I know people who feel guilty for being happy when others are sad, even though the sadness was not caused by anything they did or anything they could influence. Whatever it is, if it is out of your control, it is not up to you to control it. There is no need to feel guilty.

You may feel guilty when you think you could have, or should have, done more, better, or different. If the situation is past, and therefore unchangeable, feeling guilt does not serve a purpose. You can resolve to do more, better, or different the next time you are in a similar situation. But you can't change the past. To feel better, you can reassure yourself that you did what you could with the knowledge and resources you had at the time. Knowledge and ability are often earned through experience. As Maya Angelou famously said, "I did then what I knew how to do. Now that I know better, I do better."

It is also okay to allow yourself to feel better.

If you have truly wronged someone, find the courage to apologize and to ask for forgiveness. If you have come to know better through the experience of doing wrong, feeling guilt, and apologizing, you owe a debt of gratitude to the person who helped you learn. Owning your mistake will make you a better person. Trust me on this one.

Giving too much weight to the opinions of others
When I was growing up, my father often told me to ignore the opinions of other people and do whatever pleased me. Of course, there was one exception to this advice. I had better pay attention to what *he* thought, or I would be in deep trouble.

His advice, while well-intentioned, didn't ring true to me. I did care what other people thought. I wanted to be liked and accepted by others. I valued their companionship, and I liked to be included in social activities. My father delivered this advice many times during my childhood, always with great emphasis. I could tell he really believed what he was saying, so I grew up believing there must be something wrong with me. I did crave the approval of others, and I could not make myself stop caring what they thought.

When I grew older, I learned acceptance by others is one of the most basic human needs. To be cut off from the tribe means to be alone and in danger of being eaten by wild animals or killed by members of another tribe. Valuing social inclusion is instinctive in humans, not maladaptive. We only get into trouble when we pay attention only to what others think or say while completely factoring out our own opinions or desires.

Other people will often tell you what they think, what they value, and what they believe you should do. I think you should buy copies of this book for every person you know and even buy extra copies to hand out to strangers on the street. I say this because I think my own advice is pretty good, and heaven knows I will enjoy having the money.

This example illustrates what you need to be aware of when listening to the opinions of others. They may not always have your best interests at heart. Even if they are somewhat concerned with your interests, they may have needs of their own they are addressing. This may not be as obvious as reaping profits from book sales. Sometimes, what others want is to feel superior to you or even to outright hurt you by making you doubt your own thoughts and feelings. Bullying doesn't end at the schoolyard, and you don't have to participate in someone else's agenda.

I believe it is helpful to seek the opinions of others when you need their expertise or simply when you want to fit in socially. Just remember to keep your own counsel as well. Make decisions based on what feels right to you, combined with the information you have gathered. Ask yourself how trustworthy the opinion is and stay aware that others may be serving their own interests instead of, or in addition to, yours.

Comparing yourself to others

A friend recently attended a seminar and struck up a conversation with the presenter during the lunch break. She was impressed by the woman's resume, which featured high-profile jobs, including serving as a dean at two different colleges. She also held several advanced degrees and had raised thirteen—count 'em—thirteen children! I immediately thought of my own accomplishments and how they stacked up against those of this superwoman. I had a few entry-level jobs and one fairly good job before becoming a full-time, stay-at-home mom. I raised two children. I did manage to complete a bachelor's degree at a local college at the age of thirty-three, but I never did much with it. The end.

I concluded that I am a slacker.

My friend, who is devoted to practicing the healthy thinking habits of A Decided Difference, jumped all over me. She pointed out that, as a dean of colleges, the advanced degrees were more easily attainable for the woman and probably came with free tuition. If the woman worked full-time, she asked, how much attention could each of those thirteen children have possibly received? She also pointed out that I had no way of knowing what kind of help and resources she had. She closed by saying if I didn't stop calling myself a slacker, she would have to take matters into her own hands. I got the message.

Author Marjorie Holmes wrote, "Let me remember that each life must follow its own course, and that what happens to other people has absolutely nothing to do with what happens to me."

My values and experiences are different from those of the woman with the very many degrees and the very many children. My values and experiences are different from those of the friend who made me stop saying I was a slacker. My values and experiences are different from yours, and yours are different from those of everyone else. This is what makes you who you are and what makes the world endlessly interesting and worth exploring.

I know I have helped many people clarify their thinking. I have provided value to family members, friends, clients, audience members, podcast listeners, and strangers I will never meet. I get to choose my behavior each and every day of my life, and you do, too. The best thing you can bring to the world is your own self. Comparing yourself to others is a pointless activity, whether you believe you are worse or better than they are. You are the only you that ever was or will ever be.

Don't get me wrong. I think it is fine to look at another person's accomplishments and say, "I want that for myself, too." I also think it's fine to look at another person's failures and say, "I don't want that for myself." We can all learn from another's experiences, but making the judgment that you are better or worse than another person serves no useful purpose. It only disconnects you from others, whether you see yourself as superior or as unrealistically small.

Assuming there are only two choices in any given situation

The world is divided into two kinds of people: those who divide the world into two kinds of people, and those who don't. How many times have you seen or heard a statement like that? Our culture is filled with references to dividing things into two categories. One of the first things we teach our children is the concept of opposites. We divide our world into male/female, positive/negative, hot/cold, up/down, inside/outside, dark/light, right/left, right/wrong. We ask, "Are you in or are you out? Is the answer yes or no?" We love our black and white, dualistic thinking patterns and try to avoid gray areas, because it seems so much easier. While this way of thinking may look simpler on the surface, insisting there are only two choices can cause us untold problems.

If you believe you have to be completely happy, without a hint of grief, disappointment, or anxiety for it to count as true happiness, you will make yourself miserable. If you believe you either make the right choice or the wrong one, you prevent yourself from taking risks that could lead to excellent outcomes in the future.

The world has plenty of yes-or-no, right-or-wrong circumstances, but there are more situations where multiple options exist. When you force yourself into making a choice because you think there are only two options, you cut yourself off from much potential happiness and success. If you are torn between two lovers, or two jobs, or two houses, or two anythings, and you just can't make a decision, consider whether either of the options feel right to you. Maybe there is a third, or a fifth, or a sixteenth choice that would lead you to a better conclusion. Maybe the time is not right to make a choice at all, and if you can avoid rushing to choose, a better alternative will appear. It's possible you could combine two or more alternatives or take a different path altogether. I know someone who couldn't decide whether to become a writer or an artist. Now, she is a registered nurse who loves her work. If she had not been open to exploring her options, she might still be stuck.

Making negative predictions about the future
When you look down the road ahead, what do you see? None of us can foretell the future with one-hundred percent accuracy, but that doesn't stop us from trying. When you make plans for the future, your brain's negativity bias will automatically kick in if you don't actively take steps to neutralize it.

Imagine you are single and you want to ask an attractive person out for coffee. Are you gleefully imagining he or she will respond with an enthusiastic yes? Or are you visualizing yourself slinking away after being rejected, having to find ways to avoid seeing that person in the future? If you make the negative prediction and dwell on the bad outcome you might get, you will prevent yourself from asking in the first place. Of course, as we have just said, there are third and fourth options and more. He or she might say no but be open to yes at a later date. He or she might say yes and then cancel. He or she might say no because of fear of being a terrible conversation partner. Or they might say yes and actually be a disappointing date, rather than the engaging person you anticipated.

The point is, you can't know in advance what is going to happen, especially when other people have a choice in how to respond. You can research, and plan, and prepare, and your store may still flop. You can wing giving a speech and get a rousing response. You can't always predict how things will turn out, but you can depend on your brain coming up with every possible way you could fail.

I am not advocating taking foolish risks or investing your money carelessly or giving your heart recklessly to the first cute guy or gal who comes along. Things can and do go wrong, even when you do everything you can to plan for contingencies. What I am saying is to give yourself permission to take some risks rather than always playing it safe, knowing that if things don't work out, you can bounce back from failure. You can cope if you choose to, and you just might succeed and then build on your success.

Taking things personally when they are not personal
When I was young, I worked for a boss who was unpredictable and touchy. His behavior was erratic. He would be warm and engaging one day, short and snappish the next. He could be charming and affable in the morning

but impatient and insulting in the late afternoon. When I first started in that job, I tried to figure out what I was doing to set him off and how to stop doing it. Even though I was new in the position, I avoided asking him for help or even clarification about my assignments. I hid my disappointment when assignments I dearly wanted went to others who didn't care about them one way or the other. Inwardly, I was hurt when he ignored my good work, and I seethed with anger when he criticized me unfairly. Outwardly, I behaved as though I was as malleable as clay, dependably ready to accommodate whatever mood he happened to inhabit at any given moment. I was miserable, and I couldn't stop wondering if he enjoyed belittling me.

After a few weeks on the job, I had a conversation with a more experienced co-worker who complained he was not getting assignments he dearly wanted. The boss ignored his good work and criticized him unfairly. He had decided to look for another job, rather than to keep accommodating the boss's capricious moods. My eyes were suddenly opened. Because I was new and feeling out of my depth in the job, I had not noticed that the boss treated everyone the same way he treated me. I was taking it personally, when it wasn't personal at all.

You are the center of your own universe. Some people will criticize you for having this perspective, but you have no other choice. You can only see the world from your own perspective. Yes, you can have empathy and imagine yourself in another's situation, but you can't truly occupy their place. It is normal to think first of yourself in any given circumstance, and that was what I had been doing at work. I thought the boss's behavior was about me, because let's face it—my whole life is about me, just as your whole life is about you.

When you can depersonalize criticism or lack of recognition, it becomes much easier to handle. When something painful or frustrating arises in your life, ask yourself if it is truly about you or just part of the common experience shared by all. If it is not personal, then please don't take it that way. If it is directed at you personally, you still have choices. You can decide to ignore it, to fight it, to compromise with it, to escape from it, or to handle it in any way you choose. You don't have to feel bad, whether it is personal or not.

Pleasing others but not pleasing yourself
Although this is frequently seen as primarily a women's issue, men struggle with this as well. It's true that girls often grow up encouraged to be caretakers, tending to the needs of others before they tend to their own. This cultural pressure is lighter now than it was in the immediate post-war years of the 1950s, but it remains in subtle and not-so-subtle forms.

Pleasing other people often feels wonderful. I love taking action to care for my daughters, even though they are adults who are fully capable of taking care of themselves. It feels great to be needed and appreciated, whether by family members, friends, or even strangers. The problem with pleasing others occurs when you neglect your own needs in order to take care of others who may or may not need your caretaking. Even if you are caring for a family member who is bedridden and clearly in need, you will burn out and may fall into depression if you ignore your own needs completely.

Martyrdom is not required for you to be a good person. Self-sacrifice may be noble, at least in the short term, but it is not sustainable. Taking care of yourself is a requirement if you are to have the strength and energy to take care of anyone else. I will spare you the oxygen-mask-on-an-airplane analogy, because you already know it, but I will say you cannot share from an empty cup.

It is not wrong to take care of others, but it is also right to take care of yourself. That includes your emotional needs as well as physical ones for nutrition, recreation, and sleep. Taking time to read a good book, or get a relaxing massage, or spend time with friends will help you feel refreshed and ready to go back to whatever demands life places on you.

If you are taking care of people who are fully capable of taking care of themselves, you might want to examine your motives or the benefits you get from doing it. It does feel good to feel needed, but creating dependency in someone else in order to make yourself happy is not healthy. Consider finding a helping role where your skills are really needed, such as in a day care center, nursing home, or other volunteer capacity. These ways of fulfilling your need to be needed are healthier choices, and they just might lead you to new interests that will expand your enjoyment of life.

Ignoring your physical body
This is a common action that grows out of thinking you don't deserve, don't have time, or aren't able to take care

of yourself. If you are staggering around exhausted, out of shape, and underfed or overweight, chances are your emotional health is suffering as well. One of my favorite unhealthy coping mechanisms is eating sugary foods when life is less than sweet. I know I am not coping well when the number on the scale starts to creep up and the waistbands of my pants get tighter. When you feel depressed or anxious, you may go in the opposite direction, losing your appetite and growing too thin.

Insomnia is a common issue for people coping with anxiety, because we tend to stay awake at night, unable to relax while running what-if scenarios in our minds. We worry and fret over what might happen or ruminate over past hurts or mistakes or losses. When I was depressed, I wanted to sleep all the time, because escaping into sleep gave me relief from my negative feelings. Staying in bed too long made me feel draggy, and I also neglected some of my responsibilities, which only made me feel more worthless.

Using alcohol or drugs to numb feelings is hard on your physical body as well. It may even lead to illness or injury. It's ironic that the physical things we do to make ourselves feel better in the moment can come with such a high cost in the long run.

Our physical bodies are quite resilient, but abuse and neglect take their toll over time. If you think your body will forgive you for poor nutrition, substance abuse, lack of exercise, and lack of sleep, you will be right, but only for a while. Choosing to feed yourself nutritious foods, exercise your body, get adequate sleep, and avoid harmful substances will not only make you feel better physically, but mentally and emotionally as well. When you feel better emotionally, it becomes easier and more pleasant to eat nutritious foods, exercise your body, get adequate sleep, and avoid harmful substances. Taking care of your physical body, even when you don't feel like it at first, can set off a healthy cycle that reinforces itself with time and practice.

Feeling unworthy

Human brains are designed to see differences and to divide the whole world into categories. Some of the most popular categories are good/bad and right/wrong. Making judgments about what is good or right and bad or wrong is part of everyday life. The habit of thinking is deeply ingrained, even to the point that you may be making this kind of judgment call without even being aware of it.

This behavior might be all right if you are trying to choose between salad and potato chips or between water and soda, but when it comes to judging behavior, things get a lot messier. This is especially true of judging your own behavior and deciding what you "deserve."

Do you think you don't deserve to be happy because of something you did or failed to do, whether in the recent or distant past? Do you refuse to let yourself be happy until you have "earned it"? Do you think you deserve to suffer because you haven't done things perfectly, or because you have taken too long to do something, or because you let someone down? Are you constantly looking for reasons to deny yourself enjoyment of your own life because you are never good enough in your own eyes?

Do these things seem ridiculous when you see them written out on the page? So many of us engage in this way of thinking, but we are not conscious of doing it. Writing out your thoughts is a great way to become conscious of them and to begin to question and change them. Thinking you don't deserve to be happy often boils down to punishing yourself severely for a crime you didn't commit or for something that wasn't a crime in the first place.

Thinking you "should" do, be, or think certain ways
What does happiness look like to you? What does it mean to enjoy life? Is happiness something you can find any time, or is it limited to weekends, holidays, and vacations? Have you given deliberate thought to happiness, or do you just take in the messages other people give you without questioning them?

There are plenty of messages around, many of them coming from people who want to sell you something. One message I see repeatedly is that enjoyment equals having fun, and having fun equals being happy. Lying on the beach with a little umbrella drink in your hand, playing golf, snow skiing, or going to casinos are supposed to be fun. You might find the beach boring, or you play golf because it's expected in your business. I don't know about you, but snow skiing and gambling both scare me. What is fun and enjoyable for one person might be torture for another. Conversely, you may find much happiness and satisfaction in hobbies or volunteer work that place great demands on your skills and energy.

We also get the message that we should draw satisfaction from being with family. Some of the people in your family may indeed put the "fun" in functional, but I know of plenty of family situations which are anything but enjoyable. Maybe your idea of happiness is avoiding spending time with your family. A friend recently remarked about an advertisement she had seen in which a business owner bragged about treating customers like family. She laughed and said, "Nope! I'm not going there!"

It's your life. You get to decide what creates happiness for you.

Overestimating dangers

How many times have you worried about something that never even happened? How much do you worry about things like flying, visiting a strange city alone, or trying something new while others are watching? What are you afraid will happen? Do you stop yourself from taking risks because you are fearful? What potential benefits are you missing because you are afraid?

On the flip side, can you think of a time when you did dare to do something that felt risky or scary but it ended up being a good experience?

I'm a careful person. I'm not about to advise you to take up motorcycle racing or bungee jumping or rock climbing. But I will advise you to go for it if you want to try yoga, or square dancing, or public speaking. Any activity that looks like fun or an interesting challenge has the potential to broaden your experience of life and make you happier, but you have to be willing to try it.

A useful technique when you are fearful is to imagine the worst-case scenario and figure out exactly how awful it could be. Let's say you want to try bicycling with a group of friends. What are your fears? Do you think you will be left behind because you are too slow, or you'll have a stroke, or you'll get hit by a car? What is the worst case?

Now, ask yourself how likely it really is that the worst case would occur. They are your friends, so they probably won't leave you all alone. You could have a stroke sitting in front of the television. If you are riding in a group, being hit by a car is unlikely.

Now, ask yourself what the benefits would be if you go for it. You will have a good time with people you like, you will get exercise and fresh air, and you will have conquered a fear.

Most of the things we worry about never happen. How much happier could you be if you stopped being afraid to try new things?

Not trusting your own judgment

I was once in a romantic relationship with a man who frequently said things to make me doubt my own perceptions, memory, and judgment. It was terrible to feel off-balance, wondering if the way I saw things was inaccurate. When I made the decision to trust myself, the relationship fell apart. That turned out to be one of the greatest blessings of my life.

If others in your life are constantly criticizing you, there are a couple of possibilities to consider. Maybe you are a terrible person with awful judgment, or maybe you are surrounded by critics who need to put you down in order to build themselves up.

I used to spend time with people who put down my tastes, my hobbies, and my fashion sense. One in particular used to offer me unsolicited advice on how I could better myself, starting with giving up nearly everything I enjoyed eating, participating in painful exercise, and keeping my opinions to myself. When I paid attention to how this person interacted with others, I saw she was controlling to the point of domineering and would drop friends who didn't obey her suggestions.

If you doubt your own judgment, ask yourself why you feel you can't trust yourself. Are others criticizing you or do you feel you should always be able to predict outcomes? Have you been fooled by someone who lied to you or fallen prey to someone who took advantage of you? If so, how might you learn from those experiences in order to avoid repeating them?

Only you know what is most important and valuable to you. If the things you want do not involve hurting anyone else, let yourself have what you want, and trust your own judgment in making your own decisions. If you make a mistake, so what? Do your best, learn from your mistakes, and move on.

Sleepwalking through life

It is easy to fall into a rut when you go through your daily routines. You can get into the habit of getting up, going to work, shuttling kids to activities, making dinner, watching television, and going to bed, only to repeat those habits day after day after day. You daydream about the weekends, or maybe your annual family trip to the beach, but most of the time, you are just moving through your routine unconsciously. It's like you are sleepwalking, just going through the motions as you try to get from one day to the next.

This behavior is habitual, but like any habit, it can be broken. Anything you do to interrupt the routine can improve your mood and your enjoyment of life. A house I once lived in had an uncovered clerestory window that faced my bed. I began waking frequently with the sunrise, which was definitely a new behavior for night-owl me. I started the habit of reading first thing when I wake up, which sets a good tone for my day. I enjoy the intellectual stimulation of new ideas or the rejuvenation I get from reading inspirational material. You might rise earlier to go for a walk or to meditate before the rest of the household stirs. You might set aside time in the evenings to do something you enjoy, instead of vegging in front of the TV. Can you find time during the day to get out into nature? Spending time in nature is a proven mood booster, even for those who don't consider themselves outdoorsy. Something as simple as placing a houseplant on your desk can even be a day brightener.

Don't think you have to do something huge or extravagant to wake from your sleepwalk. Make a conscious decision to give someone a compliment or do something small but thoughtful, and follow through. You will make your day better as well as theirs. One of my favorite things to do when I feel blue is to drive through a fast food place for a meal or iced tea and pay for the person in line behind me. It makes me happy, and it usually makes the cashier happy. I hope it makes the recipient happy, although part of the fun is driving away before they find out what I have done. It's easy and inexpensive, but it makes me feel like a million bucks.

Accepting negative thoughts without questioning them

If I could convince you to take only one action, this would be it: start paying attention to the negative thoughts you have and challenge them. This was the first step I took to lift myself out of depression, and it is the one I immediately return to if I find my mood slipping.

Self-criticism definitely falls into this category, but so do the random negative thoughts that flicker through your mind. It's easy to find fault with others or with your situation at any given moment. It's easy to hear some piece of news and immediately assume the worst. Negative thinking patterns that have been developed and reinforced after years or even decades of habitual use are not easily vanquished. Keep in mind that even if you continue to have negative thoughts, you have not failed. Catching yourself and correcting course may happen hundreds or thousands of times, but it will be worth the effort. Consciously choosing positive thoughts can become an automatic habit, too, but you have to deliberately practice at first.

Any time you find yourself thinking something such as, "Just my luck for things to go wrong," or "There are no good men left," or "I'll never find another job as good as this one," immediately question the assumptions. Is it true, objectively true, that you always have bad luck? Is there not one good single guy left in the whole wide world? Is the job you currently hold the best you can do? Replace the negative thoughts with positive ones that are (or could be) objectively true. Think of a time when you had good luck, or remind yourself that your sister married a good guy, or imagine the person holding the job you want has just decided to retire.

Remember that the world is full of good things, good people, and good situations just waiting for you to come along. Remember to look for the good. You are unlikely to find an Easter egg if you only look for jack-o-lanterns.

Taking responsibility for things that are not within your control

Before you start feeling guilty for not controlling something, ask yourself if it really is within your ability to control it. You would not feel responsible for making the sun shine today, or for making the stock market go up, or even for choosing what I am going to have for lunch. So why would you feel responsible for your daughter's choice of boyfriends, or your husband's choice to drink six beers every night, or your mother's decision to spend her rent money on shoes? You might wish you could influence these people to make better choices. But the fact is you only have control of two things: your thoughts and your behavior.

If you feel guilty because your adult children are unhappy, or because you think you should have married your college boyfriend, or because you should have known better than to do something, you are wasting your time as well as making yourself feel terrible. It is not within your power to make someone else happy. No one can change the past, and no one "should" know better. We do the best we can, with the knowledge and resources we have, at the time we are in.

Rather than beating yourself up for failing to control circumstances or another person, choose to focus on those things you can control and that are your responsibility. You can set a good example to try to influence another person, but the choice of whether to emulate your behavior is up to them. Your job is to choose thoughts and behavior that are worth emulating and make yourself as happy and satisfied as possible in the process.

Choosing discouraging language
Are you depressed (a state of being) or discouraged (a temporary feeling)? Words matter! Happiness is not about making a one-time decision that cures depression. Happiness is a series of decisions, and one of the most important you can make is to choose appropriate language. Choosing words that are accurate, specific, and encouraging can make a great difference in how you feel about yourself, others, and the situations you find yourself in.

A subtle but important distinction you can make is to choose language that is positively phrased instead of phrasing that contains a negative. This is not about "positive thinking." It is about avoiding words which carry a negation, such as not or never. A long-held psychological tenet says the subconscious mind cannot understand a negative and will ignore the presence of a negative when it hears one. For example, telling yourself, "I will not forget where I put my keys," is heard by your subconscious as the instruction, "I will forget where I put my keys." As

I said, the distinction is quite subtle, but choosing to say, "I will remember where I put my keys," may help ensure you will spend less time looking for them.

Deliberately choosing this type of phrasing can, over time, change your attitude about how much control you have over your life. If you say you are not going to do something, and then you do it, you may blame yourself for failing or punish yourself with guilt or regret. More positive phrasing helps you set an intention for the type of behavior you will engage in, rather than focusing your attention what you will try to avoid. Whatever you focus on becomes more prominent in your mind. Focusing on desired behavior will help you see more opportunities to find or create what you want.

Believing failure is always negative

A few years before the completion of this book, my husband and I started having serious problems in our marriage. I was not interested in another divorce; I was determined this marriage would succeed. I had married my first husband twice (yes, twice) and spent a total of 22 years with him. When I married my second husband after two years of dating, I was certain I had finally gotten it right. Seven years later, my happily married identity was revealed to be based on an illusion—but it would take me almost three years to decide to file for divorce.

It took me so long because I could hardly bear the thought of another failure. As I navigated the process of trying to find or create solutions, I allowed myself to think of divorce only as the last possible resort. I worked on myself and hoped for a miracle, but eventually I had to consider that divorce might be the only option that would allow me to move forward in a healthy fashion.

I consulted with Jim, my long-time counselor. He suggested I reframe the way I looked at divorce. He said, "You may have had failed marriages, but you have not failed at marriage." While I hoped what he said was true (that I had done everything I could have done in both situations), what helped the most was asking myself what I could learn from the relationships. In doing this, I began to understand that success often comes cloaked in what looks like initial failure.

By examining my actions and their results, I saw patterns of behavior that helped me understand myself and the situations. I recognized how I had postponed or abandoned seeking my own goals, my hopes and dreams, to try to save relationships that turned out to be unsalvageable. As I began to understand my role in the dysfunction, I could choose better options going forward.

It is possible to use failure as a springboard to a larger success. While failing is painful, and I would prefer to avoid it, there is not a more effective teacher. If you can find the courage to examine your failures, you may find the seeds of future successes. You may also find enough manure to fertilize them!

Thinking small changes are not worthwhile

I took up running when I was in my late thirties, mainly because I hung out with a group of women who were runners. I wanted to spend time with them, and I wanted to identify as a runner. Never mind that I had never exhibited any discernible athletic ability. In fact, when I was in middle school, I couldn't even run all the way around the quarter-mile track. At the age of 37 I could barely walk five blocks without being exhausted, but I listened when one of the ladies told me she had started walking for exercise. She decided to run instead because she was a busy physician with three small children and walking just took too much time. I didn't really believe I could become a runner, but I started walking anyway. After a few weeks, I started adding brief bursts of jogging to my walks: a block here, two blocks there. One thrilling day, I ran a half-mile. A few days later, I ran eight-tenths of a mile, and I felt ready to run a full mile. When the time came, I returned to the middle school track, the site of my childhood humiliation, and ran around that hated track four times without stopping. That first full mile still stands out in my mind as one of the greatest accomplishments of my life.

Eventually, by adding a little more effort here and a little more distance there, I worked up to running 13.1 miles, a half-marathon. It was a huge change for a woman who could barely walk five blocks, but it happened a little bit at a time—step by step.

You can achieve results of the same magnitude by changing your ways of thinking a little at a time. One of my good friends used to have crippling anxiety and regularly took medication to manage it. She had good reasons to feel concerned about her situation and her future, but worrying makes not one whit of positive difference in how things turn out for anyone. In fact, worrying can make things much worse, because ruminating over what might happen depletes your mental energy. It wastes mental resources that could be applied to finding real-world solutions.

In listening to her, I realized how frequently she used the word "anxious," especially when she meant to express anticipating something good. She would say things such as, "I'm anxious to get to see my daughter when she comes home to visit," or "I'm anxious for my vacation week to get here." I started to point out the word "anxious" when I heard her using it in that way, and I suggested she substitute the word "eager" instead. She could also have chosen to say she was excited or keen for something to happen.

By making this one simple change, she started to notice the difference between feeling tense and worried or alive and excited. By merely decreasing her use of the word "anxious," she substantially reduced her anxiety levels. By combining this practice with other healthy thinking techniques, she was able to manage her moods without medication, even as she navigated difficult family situations and a challenging new job.

Believing in fate or destiny

If you believe you are not in control of your life, you never will be. If you believe whatever happens to you is tied to a predetermined outcome, then it doesn't much matter what you do. This belief is a double-edged sword. If you reach a goal you have set for yourself, it means fate was on your side and you couldn't have failed, so you don't get to take much pride in whatever you accomplished. After all, if it was bound to happen, how could you claim credit? Conversely, if you work hard to accomplish something which ultimately eludes you, it must not have been meant to be. Why, then, would you work so hard in the first place?

This belief can create the worst of both worlds. You have no control, so why try? We look at whatever has happened and call it fate or destiny, even when at the outset there was no way to predict the outcome. We humans tend to see what happens and then use our 20/20 hindsight to explain why. Foresight tends to be substantially less perfect.

Waiting until the time is right or until you "deserve" to be happy

Do you believe you can't be happy until something specific happens? Have you ever heard someone (maybe yourself) say, "I'll be happy when _____?" Fill in the blank. When . . . I graduate from high school, get my degree, get a new job, find my soul mate, get married, have a child, get a promotion, finish raising kids, pay for the kids' college, retire. You can wait to be happy while your whole life passes by, and then you can look back with nostalgia at the good old days. Wouldn't it be better to enjoy your life now, where you are, as you are, even as you work to improve? Waiting for the perfect time or perfect circumstances to be happy practically guarantees you never will be.

My mother used to say she was waiting to have nice things until we kids grew up. My brother was eight years younger than me, and he was pretty rambunctious. By the time he moved out of the house, I was already a parent, and so was my sister. Then, my mother said she didn't want to have breakables around because the grandchildren were often at her house. The grandchildren were all adults before she finally allowed herself to update the house and buy (or bring out of storage) some pretty things she wanted to display and enjoy. I'm glad she lived long enough to do it.

No one is guaranteed to live long enough to make it until. Postponing happiness doesn't guarantee more joy tomorrow. It just guarantees less joy than you could have had today. Besides, being happy is a skill just like thinking is. The more you practice it, the better you get.

Enjoying life and working to make it better are not mutually exclusive. You can be happy today and go back to college. You can enjoy hobbies and friendships while waiting to meet your soul mate. You can enjoy your children today and save money for their future education.

Believing it is selfish to want to be happy

If you are like most people, you like to help others. It feels great to be needed and to contribute. However, when you decide to serve others at the expense of your own happiness, you do not add to the level of happiness in the world. I am not talking about sacrificing trips to Europe to pay for your child's college. Everyone has to set priorities, and paying for a child's education can feel rewarding and be satisfying. I'm talking about such things as routinely pretending you don't care where to go for dinner or what to do on the weekend, or acting like it doesn't matter whether you get a needed new coat when your spouse wants to buy an expensive new electronic toy. If you are racking up credit card debt to give your kid the latest designer clothes, you aren't doing either one of you any favors.

There is a difference between ranking priorities and making yourself a martyr. Occasionally acquiescing and saying, "Whatever you want," may be necessary in the give and take of a loving relationship or a friendship. But if you never get a turn to choose, you are bound to feel resentful eventually. I know women who completely lost track of what they liked after years of complying with overbearing husbands, and men who did the same to appease their wives. But I also know spouses who would have been happier with a more equitable arrangement. If you think you are being noble by sacrificing your own happiness, ask yourself how you would feel if your spouse, or parent, or child put themselves in the same position in order to "make" you happy. You do not contribute to the light of the world by choosing to sit in darkness.

If you continue to struggle with the idea that choosing to be happy is selfish, remember this: Scientific research has found moods to be contagious within human groups, whether they are families, classmates, friends, or colleagues. While you may think choosing your own happiness is selfish behavior, you probably want others to be happy (as long as it isn't at your expense). If you bring your negative mindset, unhappiness, or even depression into the groups you belong to, you could be responsible for bringing all the members down. Conversely, by being cheerful and joyful, you spread the seeds of happiness for others. When you see it this way, you understand that being unhappy is actually the more selfish choice.

You may find other errors in your thinking that are worthy of challenge and change. When you do, I hope you celebrate your increased self-awareness and your willingness to grow. As human beings, we are designed to continue to grow throughout our lives. Growth only happens when you are willing to let go of the old to make room for the new.

You do not deserve to be depressed or anxious. You deserve the best life you can create for yourself. Be willing, be aware, be active, and you will find yourself in a better place now and for years to come.

Continuing the Journey
Questions and actions for moving forward

- Recognize that your collection of mental habits has mostly formed unconsciously. If you have a large collection of beliefs to discard or change, be gentle with yourself.
- Changing one habit described in this chapter can make it easier to change others. Choose just one to work on at first and then build on that foundation.
- Come back to this chapter and read it again when you find yourself slipping into old patterns. You may notice something upon rereading that escaped your notice the first or second or tenth time through. Remember, your RAS will screen out information it deems irrelevant at the time.
- Thinking is a skill and can be improved with practice. So practice!

— Chapter 9 —
This Changes Everything

Friedrich Nietzsche said, "That which does not kill us makes us stronger." I wish that were always true, but I have seen many people weakened by difficult circumstances who never truly recovered their original strength, much less became stronger than before. In numerous other cases, though, people go through difficult times, including illness, financial ruin, or trauma, and do end up stronger. They thrive in the long run and frequently say the tragedies in their lives turned out to be invaluable learning opportunities. It's true that blessings can come heavily disguised.

You have heard of PTSD (Post-Traumatic Stress Disorder), but have you heard about post-traumatic growth? Whether a person experiences a single traumatic event or ongoing trauma, such as repeated abuse or living in a war zone, that person is not doomed to suffer forever after. What makes some people flourish after enormous challenges while others flounder and sink in the face of the same situations? By now, you won't be surprised by my answer. It is because they make the conscious choice to become stronger through learning from their challenges, problems, and even disasters.

You can learn powerful lessons from others when you look at what they have done in the face of overwhelming odds. There has rarely been a time in my life when, facing a serious problem of some kind, I have not reached for a book or conducted online research for advice from those who have been there. There is no substitute for first-hand experience that has led to triumph. Those who have been there are the guides I want to follow. This is the kind of guide I have tried to be for you in this book.

If you take only one thing away from this book, I hope you will remember that you always have a choice in any situation, even if the choice is to think about it in a different way. You can't always change the circumstances the world throws at you, but you can choose to see yourself as strong, capable, and flexible in responding to the demands put upon you.

You can choose the new thinking patterns you want to develop and strengthen through conscious practice. You can choose which new habits you will build through repetition. You can decide how to conduct your thoughts and your behaviors and thereby create your emotions. You can choose deliberate rehearsal of the methods of healthy thinking until they become automatic.

These are habits I suggest you build into your daily life. One, discover what brings you joy and satisfaction, not just pleasure or relaxation. Two, give yourself compliments and credit on a regular basis, not just when you do something that seems extraordinary. And three, tell yourself better stories that cast you as a hero who is able to cope with whatever comes your way.

Discovering what brings you joy and satisfaction is transformative. Keep in mind that you may need to start small. Carry a small notebook with you or create a note on your phone. Jot down a reminder every time you do or encounter something that makes you smile, light up with happiness, or feel a sense of satisfaction. This exercise is all about you. No one else has to see your list, so make it as real as you possibly can. There is no reason to feel ashamed or embarrassed by what you like (unless it hurts you or someone else or is illegal or immoral). I like walking in the sunshine, riding my bicycle, and reading in bed. None of these are going to set the world on fire, but so what? They light a comforting fire in my heart— and that's what matters. I find a sense of satisfaction in regularly cleaning out and organizing my closets. That may seem a bit odd to others, but again, so what? I have nice closets and a smile on my face. I like to cook, and crochet, and sew. Unlike most of the population, I also love to give speeches. Do you think that last one is kind of bizarre? If you do, and I mean this in the nicest way possible, I don't care.

Allow yourself to not only discover what you like, but also to indulge in it as often as possible. The one task you cannot outsource is enjoying your own life.

If and when you start to feel selfish for giving yourself the time, the space, the money, and the permission to enjoy yourself, remember what Robert Louis Stevenson wrote about happiness. "There is no duty that we so much underrate as the duty of being happy. By being happy we sow anonymous benefits upon the world." Happy people are smilers and givers. They brighten the days of those they encounter. The benefits happy people create can pass from one person to another to another. The world is a better place when you are happier in it.

Giving yourself credit and compliments guarantees you will have a regular source of positive input. If you wait for others to notice your awesomeness and comment on it, you may go hungry for positive reinforcement on a regular basis. It may feel weird and uncomfortable at first, especially if your habit is to comment on your perceived flaws and faults in your effort to make improvements. Hush the inner critic and try going the complimentary route for a while. See if you don't get better results. Smile at yourself in the mirror and tell yourself something good. It can be as simple as a positive comment about your appearance or as significant as congratulating yourself for winning a Nobel prize. It all counts, and it all matters. You will not become a conceited, puffed-up egomaniac if you do this. You will become a person who regularly looks for the good things in yourself and others and who comments on those good things. You will become someone everybody likes to be around, including yourself.

Casting yourself as the hero in your stories will not turn you into an unbearable braggart, either. Your inner stories determine how you will show up in life: ready to tackle problems head on and thrive, or shrink down and hope someone else will step up to cover your weakness. Seeing yourself as someone who can cope, no matter what life throws at you, turns you into someone who can cope, no matter what life throws at you. Telling better stories means seeing the positives in yourself, but it also means deciding to reject ideas that don't serve you. It means setting boundaries to protect your mental health. You can decide not to take things personally, especially when they are not personal. You can choose not to take responsibility for things you cannot control. You can stop making negative predictions about the future. These are your stories. You get to decide what they say and how they make you feel.

As I was nearing the end of the writing of this book, my decade-long marriage to my second husband finally fell apart after three years of struggle. I couldn't help thinking how ironic the timing was. It seemed custom tailored to torpedo my self-confidence and happiness at a particularly vulnerable time. It was very important for me to take control of my stories.

I knew I had done everything in my power to save the marriage, but failing that, I had to save myself. Even though I knew that, the old patterns of fear and self-doubt sent out tentacles into my heart and brain as soon as my husband packed up his things and left. The inner critic immediately went crazy. "No one will want your book now," she sneered. "Fat chance anyone will want advice from a woman who has failed at marriage the way you have. You had better hope your rental property keeps producing income for you, because no one will want to read or listen to your work anymore. Who wants advice from a failure?"

I spent a goodly amount of time crying the first few

weeks. The poor little girl who lives deep inside me woke me up crying in the night, worried she couldn't take care of herself and would die alone and lonely. Anxiety colored my daily experience. I fretted about money and loneliness, and I worried my friends would start to see me as a burden if I leaned on them too much. In a few dark moments, I imagined that no one would ever love me again.

Once, when I was messaging with a friend, I told him I was having a rough day. He responded with, "None of your own stuff is working, eh?" "On the contrary," I told him. "It works. I just happen to be using it to stay afloat instead of drowning at this particular time."

There are times when it is impossible to be completely happy. There are times of grief, when feelings of loss and sadness overwhelm us. Although times of sadness are inevitable, it does not follow that depression will always return. I characterized my sadness as normal, which it was, and myself as capable of coping, which I am. Viewing myself and my situation through this lens meant I could experience my grief and sadness without having to be afraid it would never abate. I knew the crying spells would get shorter and farther apart. I knew I would manage financially, because I would do whatever I had to do. I knew that being alone does not necessarily equate to being lonely. It was up to me to choose how to tell the stories I told myself. I could play the hero or the victim, and I would live up or down to the role I gave myself. By now, you surely know which I chose. As I navigated the shoals of emotions and legalities, I kept in mind that I was responsible for choosing the attitudes that would create my thoughts and feelings. Did I always feel strong and powerful? Uh, no. But I also did not feel weak and at the mercy of others or of the world at large. I knew how to modulate my negative emotions through my practice of healthy thinking. And when I did fall off the track, I knew how to get back on, and I did so as quickly as possible.

I have been on the Decided Difference path for sixteen years at this writing, and I still find the methods I have described in this book useful in keeping my spirits high and my outlook positive. Yes, I still have bad days sometimes. Yes, I still have to choose to examine my thinking for errors and tell myself better stories. And yes, it is always worth the effort.

One recent morning, I woke up to a gray winter day which I knew was going to be quite cold. My muscles felt stiff and sore after exercise I had done the day before. My joints and my back hurt. My body and brain do not transition from sleep to wakefulness very easily, and I am grouchy when I first wake up. As I lay there, considering whether to get out of my warm bed, my thoughts automatically drifted downward. I hate overcast days, and I hate cold, and I hate hurting, and I hate feeling terrible when I first wake up. All I could think about was how bad I felt, until I remembered to choose happier thoughts.

I reminded myself that once I started moving, the stiffness in my muscles and the pain in my joints would ease. I thought about how much I was going to enjoy my first cup of coffee and my breakfast. I thought of the friends I would see later in the day. I thought of how much I would enjoy working on this book while sitting in my comfortable chair in my lovely office. I thought of how many things I had to be grateful for and how many things I had to look forward to that day. The next thing I knew, my bad mood had shrunk down to nothing and had been replaced by a much sunnier outlook. I rolled out of bed, grateful for the power I have to decide how I will think and feel.

I want you to remember two words when you feel down, or discouraged, or weak, or tired of having to work so hard at this happiness thing. Keep trying. Read something uplifting or encouraging. Listen to a podcast or an audiobook that gives you a boost. You can find at least a year's worth of my podcast episodes at http://decideddifference.libsyn.com/. Call a friend. Have a good cry. Ask your heart what will make it happy in the moment, and then give it to yourself. Read through the Emergency Mood Repair Kit that follows this chapter and choose a strategy to try. Do whatever it takes. Above all, do something. Take action. A friend of mine likes to say, "Do something, even if it is wrong," because she knows mistakes can be fixed or learned from, and action is the antidote to feeling stuck.

Each year, on New Year's Day, I prepare a meal in which every dish signifies an aspiration for the year to come. The exact recipes vary somewhat from one year to the next, but the meal must contain certain traditional elements. Rice is for health, black-eyed peas are for good luck, and greens are for prosperity. The meal must also include pork, because according to Southern lore, pigs cannot look behind them.

When you begin your Decided Difference journey,

go ahead and be a pig. Don't look back. I don't care how many years you have spent depressed, or paralyzed by fear, or overwhelmed by anxiety. I don't care how long you have beaten yourself up over things you couldn't control. I don't care how long you've thought you were undeserving or felt guilty for wanting to be happy. Those years are over now. Your happiness is waiting for you to create it.

Continuing the Journey
Actions for moving forward

- Read the 10 Quick Tools for Beating Depression and Anxiety which follow this chapter. You can download a printable version at http://decideddifference.com/resources/.
- Keep trying!

A Decided Difference
Emergency Mood Repair Kit
10 Quick Tools for Beating
Depression and Anxiety

If you have thoughts of suicide or self-harm, please call for help. The number of the National Suicide Prevention Lifeline is 1-800-273-8255.

Events that we label as "negative" or "bad" happen in all of our lives. Sometimes your equilibrium is shaken by these life events. Maybe a friend or family member is diagnosed with a serious illness or dies suddenly. Maybe a natural disaster destroys your home and your sense of safety. Maybe something you see on the news scares you to your core. Maybe you become overwhelmed by the pressures of daily life and find yourself feeling hopeless.

This compact emergency kit is for use during those times when you feel you can't cope, when you feel paralyzed by anxiety, or overwhelmed by feelings of depression.

It is designed to lift you off the bottom and set you back on your feet with a renewed sense of hope.

Like any tool kit, using this one does require work. A hammer can't drive a nail without a human hand picking up the tool and swinging it. It is up to you to pick up these tools and use them. Fortunately, they can help you to feel better right away, even if they are not used perfectly.

1. **Recognize that you have a choice about how to think and feel.** Deliberately choosing your thoughts is not the same as denying your feelings. When something bad happens or you feel overwhelmed, sometimes you are instinctively angry, hurt, sad, or afraid. Negative or frustrating events happen to everyone. Circumstances change. What happens is not always within your control, but how you choose to respond is within your control. Your responses depend largely on how you think about what has happened—your internal response to the external world. You do not have to respond to external events in the same way your mother would, the way your best friend would, or the way the world says you "should." Remember, your thoughts create your feelings. Do not take this to mean you are to blame for feeling depressed or anxious. It simply means you can turn those feelings away with the right tools. Dealing with life is a requirement. Feeling miserable while doing it is optional. You can smile and deal or cry and deal. Choose one or the other, but know this: it is your choice.

2. **Be present in the present moment.** Be here, now. The thoughts provoking your bad mood are probably about something that is not happening in this present moment. You may be ruminating about things that happened this morning or last week or last year. You might worry about what will happen tonight or tomorrow or next month. Ask yourself what is bothering you. If the answer begins with "What if . . ." or "I should . . ." or "If only . . .," this strategy may be helpful. Focus on this very moment. Where are you? What are you doing? What is in your immediate environment? Are things happening right now that are pleasant? Is there something in this very moment to enjoy if you will allow yourself? The past and the future exist only in our imaginations. There is only the present moment in which to live, and you get to decide what to do with this moment. It is yours. Take it.

3. **Focus on gratitude.** This is definitely my go-to, my first choice, my all-time favorite happiness practice. It is always possible to find something to be grateful for in any circumstance, even if you simply feel grateful that a bad situation isn't worse. If you are able to look around you, be grateful for your eyes. You are able to see! Be grateful that you are safe in this moment, physically comfortable, well fed, whatever. Most of the time, you will come up with far more details to feel grateful about. It does not have to be complicated. Human brains cannot focus on gratitude and negativity at the same time. Allow your

gratitude to force out the thoughts causing your bad feelings.

4. **See yourself with compassion.** If a good friend was in your current situation, how would you treat him or her? Would you berate your friend for being weak, lazy, helpless, or pathetic? If not, why would you treat yourself that way? If you were talking to a friend, what advice would you give? How about giving yourself a break and being gentle with yourself? Remind yourself, as you would remind a friend, that whatever it is, this too shall pass.

5. **Listen to your mental soundtrack.** All of us have automatic thoughts running through our minds without conscious effort. If you make it a point to really listen to those thoughts, you may find they create an unending stream of negativity. Are the things you say to yourself inside your own head true? Or are they simply a loop of comments made by others, criticisms from the past, or your own thoughts about how you are falling short of your ideals? It is your head. You can choose to notice, challenge, and change the mental soundtrack playing in there. Review Tool #4 for suggestions about how to change it.

6. **Look for errors in your thinking.** Common, simple mistakes can lead to depressed feelings. Are you making these errors in your thinking? You may be magnifying the negatives while minimizing the positives in your life. This can drag your feelings down fast. Are you using words like always, never, should, and must in your self-talk?

Would your friends agree with the things you say to yourself? Would they talk to you that way? Writing the thoughts down can help you challenge them more easily. Ask yourself also whether having these thoughts helps you in any way. Even if what you think is "true," is it helpful to dwell upon it? St. Paul's admonition to the Corinthians—to think on things that are lovely—is still good advice 2,000 years later. Also keep in mind the tendency of depressed people to think in catastrophic and global terms. It probably isn't true that your whole life is ruined by one bad event, even if the bad event is truly terrible. You can probably think of people who have survived and thrived after worse. You can too, even if it seems impossible right now.

7. **Ask yourself, "What do I want right now?"** Yes, it is okay to ask, and it is okay to give yourself what you truly need. Individuals experiencing a depressed mood can be especially bad at answering this question. They know what their friends and loved ones want, but they have a hard time answering for themselves. I am not talking about things like, "I want world peace," or, "I want my problems with my in-laws resolved." You know those things are not within your control anyway. Look for a small answer to relieve the stress you are feeling right now. There is nothing wrong with wanting a walk in the fresh air, a nap, a funny movie, or a good cry. Your heart knows what will make it feel better. Ask.

8. **Check in with your body.** How are you feeling physically? Are you hungry? Are you overly tired or even exhausted? Are you suffering from a physical ailment such as a virus, or do you have a chronic illness that is not being well-managed? If your physical body is suffering or out of balance in some way, your mood may be blue or you may feel irritable. I have come to understand that if my body is not happy, it can wreak havoc with my mind. If my body is not well fed and well rested, it can make my mind and my heart miserable. If you aren't sure if your bad feelings originate with your body or your mind, try feeding yourself nourishing foods like fruit, vegetables, and high-quality proteins. Try soaking your muscles in a hot bath. Take a nap or get a good night's rest and see how you feel afterwards. Even if you still have problems to deal with when you wake up, things may seem better in the morning simply because you are refreshed. Refilling your physical energy reserves often gives you more mental stamina as well.

9. **Do something.** Don't just sit there—do something. Get up off the couch. Wash your face. Do anything, as long as it absorbs your mind or allows your mind to rest while your hands are busy. Cook a complicated dish or pull weeds in the garden. Go to a secondhand store and see if you can find something that reminds you of your high school years. Chase a butterfly. Clean a closet. Just make sure you do something active.

Vegging out in front of the television or the computer can make you feel worse. Human brains are not meant to be left to their own devices. Given a task, anything at all to do, the brain will get busy, for better or for worse. Give your brain something to think about besides the miserable thoughts that brought you to the mood of depression or anxiety.

10. **Keep trying.** If you try something and it works, keep doing it. Write down a reminder of what you did that worked. Write yourself a note and put it where you can find it the next time you need it. Make copies of the note and put them in multiple locations where you will see them often. If you try something and it doesn't work, then try something else, and something else, and something else, by golly, until something does work. When you find what works for you, apply it often. All these tools become easier to use and more effective with practice. Remember, thoughts cause feelings, and you really can choose your thoughts. Put your focus on lovely things, and you will see your world become a lovelier place.

About the Author

LouAnn Clark is still trying to decide whether she is a speaker who writes or a writer who speaks. When not playing with words, this proud mom of two adult daughters can be found cooking for friends, working on her goal to ride a bicycle in all fifty states, or wiggling her toes in the sand at the beach. She is probably looking for Easter eggs right now.

Visit her website at louannclark.com.

Made in the USA
Middletown, DE
15 November 2022

15106552R00086